WHO IS MY NEIGHBOUR?

Other Books by Martin Goldsmith

Life's Tapestry
Islam and Christian Witness
Jesus and His Relationships
Serving God Today
Matthew and Mission
What About Other Faiths?
God On the Move

WHO IS MY NEIGHBOUR?

World Faiths – Understanding and
Communicating

Martin Goldsmith and Rosemary Harley

Authentic
LIFESTYLE

First published in 1988 by Scripture Union
This edition published in 2002 by Authentic Lifestyle

08 07 06 05 04 03 02   7 6 5 4 3 2 1

Authentic Lifestyle is an imprint of
Authentic Media
PO Box 300, Carlisle, Cumbria, CA3 0QS, UK
and Box 1047, Waynesboro, GA 30830-2047, USA
www.paternoster-publishing.com

British Library Cataloguing in Publication Data
A catalogue record for this book is available from the British Library

ISBN 1-85078-455-8

Cover design by Campsie
Printed in Great Britain by
Cox and Wyman, Reading, Berkshire

To Elizabeth and David, our much loved and patient partners, and to all the staff at All Nations Christian College, who showed considerable tolerance while we were busy writing

Contents

PUBLISHING

OMF International works in most East Asian countries, and among East Asian peoples around the world. It was founded by James Hudson Taylor in 1865 as the China Inland Mission. Our purpose is to glorify God through the urgent evangelisation of East Asia's billions.

In line with this, OMF Publishing seeks to motivate and equip Christians to make disciples of all peoples. Publications include:

- stories and biographies showing God at work in East Asia
- the biblical basis of mission and mission issues
- the growth and development of the Church in Asia
- studies of Asian culture and religion

Books, booklets, articles and free downloads can be found on our web site at *www.omf.org*

Addresses for OMF English-speaking centres can be found at the back of this book.

1

We need to understand

The beautiful, modern Anglican church was filled to capacity. Some six hundred eager Chinese believers had gathered for their church's missionary weekend. A few Anglo-Saxon faces stood out conspicuously in the Chinese crowds. What a contrast to the average English church in which I preach!

After the service I drove home through north London with two of my Chinese friends. We crawled through a rich variety of different areas. In one we noticed that all the people were black – this was evidently a West Indian section of the city. A few streets further on we found the colour of the faces getting paler. Many of the shop names were in Urdu. Pakistanis predominated here. Then the faces became darker again as we progressed to another part of the city. The Pakistanis gave way to the equally Muslim Bangladeshis. At Stamford Hill we passed through the middle of an ultra-orthodox Jewish community. The boys wore their hair in ringlets, the men sported black beards over their black coats. Of course some traditional English faces were also to be seen – it seemed that some of the streets firmly resisted newcomers.

Who are 'the British'?

We know from our history books that Britain has always been a multiracial society. The early British tribes were driven into the far extremities of the land by the conquering Anglo-Saxons,

so it might be said that the only true Britons are to be found in
Scotland, Wales, Ireland and Cornwall! And most of those will
now have some Anglo-Saxon blood in them! Before the Anglo-
Saxons came, the Roman armies, together with their mercenar-
ies from many nations. These, too, settled in England and some
intermarried with the local population. From Scandinavia the
fierce Norsemen visited the island each year to pillage and
rape. As a result the eastern parts of England were devastated.
But gradually more and more of these ferocious seafarers settled in England, farming the land and marrying into the local
population. In 1066 a new era began. The Norman invaders
were already heavily involved in the life and politics of this
island but the fatal arrow in King Harold's eye made significant changes inevitable. With the Norman conquest French
became the language of government.

Since then, in more recent centuries, all sorts of European
immigrants have crossed the water. Germans, Dutch, Italians
and others have merged with the already mixed blood of the
British to make us what we are.

But we have to notice two significant facts about all the different races which intermingled with each other to form the
British people. Firstly, they were all white. Secondly, they all
started with animistic tribal religions, but at some stage sub-
mitted – at least nominally – to the Christian faith. Today's
immigrants are different.

Not just white

A few years ago I was talking to a West Indian student in our
college dining room. With a broad Birmingham accent she told
me that she had been born in this country and had never even
visited Jamaica where her forefathers originally came from. As
we talked further, I realized that her family had come to
Britain before mine! This came as quite a shock to me. Because
I am white and English, people do not think of me as an immigrant, whereas she is always being taken for an immigrant
because she has a deep black skin and curly West Indian hair.
But she is, in fact, as much a native of this country as I am.

Today you don't have to be white to be British, though many white people have difficulty accepting it.

Not just Christians

Only a small number of the more recent newcomers to Britain are Christian. It is true that many West Indians, increasing numbers of Chinese and some Jews, Indians and Pakistanis are Christian, but most are not. In our resident British population we now have over a million Muslims (more than all the Methodists and Baptists put together), more than 300,000 non-Christian Jews, and about 300,000 Sikhs as well as many Hindus and Buddhists. The mosque, temple and synagogue form part of the mosaic of British life.

Today you don't have to be even nominally Christian to be British.

Travel

People from all over the world have come to us here in Britain. We not only have a rich variety of people coming to settle here, but also a multitude of visitors who land on our shores each year, coming for further study, for business purposes and for sightseeing. This is of course equally true of many other countries, for fast means of travel have made the world very small. The races, cultures and religions of the world are being thrown together in an unprecedented way. It is also true that more and more British people travel abroad for long or short visits and so meet other peoples and religions on their home territory. Many of us will, at some stage, visit or work in other parts of the world: day trips to France; holidays all over the world; a year's gap between school and college that allows us to travel or work in Africa or Asia. Many firms have branches overseas or have won contracts in other countries which demand that their employees travel. Short-term mission groups like Youth With A Mission or Operation Mobilization offer young people the opportunity to work in another country for a year or two. Many of the established mission agencies also accept short-term workers, particularly if they have a professional skill to offer.

The British tourist, however, knows how to make himself feel at home overseas: fish and chips with a can of beer! Frequently we make no attempt to understand or relate to local people. But visiting or working in other parts of the world can be most enriching. If we enter into another way of life and culture we can begin to see ourselves and our own background through different eyes. Other cultures have strengths which may be lacking in our own, as well as weak areas where we may be stronger. This means that we shall learn a lot - but we may also have something to contribute.

Tensions

When different races and cultures confront each other without a desire to understand one another, to love and to relate, then severe problems can arise.

The local train journey into London starts with peaceful scenery. Ducks and moorhens swim peacefully together on the local lakes. Then the train moves into industrial zones. Graffiti on every wall assault our eyes. Like huge, poisonous spiders giant swastikas send shivers down every Jewish spine. West Indians and Asians will feel equally apprehensive for, next to the odious swastikas, large lettering shouts again and again, 'Wogs out'.

Breakfast in the university refectory. Where should I sit when I have got my tray of food? There are several tables with nothing but white students; two tables have African students; one has Chinese. All the tables are racially divided! Sitting at them are people who later in the day will join a protest against South African racialism!

An invasion of culturally different foreigners can be very threatening to any local population. They see the traditional way of life changing before their eyes. The jobs which local people feel belong to them may go to the newcomers. They might intermarry with the local population and destroy the established patterns of family life. They might even convert some of the local people to their religion. It is no wonder that such threats to a population's identity sometimes explode in racial hatred and violence. In Britain today, racial discrimination in the search for jobs and housing is all too common. In inner city areas many blacks and Asians suffer verbal abuse, as well as physical attack in the streets or even in their homes.

When I visited the Muslim country of Bangladesh, the streets of Dacca were empty of women except a few low-class workers on building sites. European tourists and world travellers stood out like city skyscrapers in a rural village. The girls were wearing shorts, publicly displaying vast areas of naked leg. I felt ashamed to be white, and shuddered at the blatant lack of cultural sensitivity which would not adjust to a foreign culture. It was offensive. No wonder many local people dislike Westerners.

But the Christian is called to love his neighbour. If we love someone we surely want to understand him. What is his background? What does he believe? What are his problems? What does he enjoy? How can we help him? Love prompts such questions. The Christian should also encourage others to love. Newcomers to Britain are often poor, needy, despised and oppressed. The Bible tells us that these people are loved by God. As his disciples, we are to be like him

Finding an identity

All of us need to know who we really are and to what groups of people we naturally belong. Immigrant peoples and their children face a significant problem in this respect. How far should they identify with their backgrounds? How far should they become like the people of the host nation and sink their identity in the ways of their new home country?

The ghetto mentality

A group of British Air Force wives once came to visit the mission centre for new missionaries, of which I was in charge, in

Singapore. I showed them round and they were fascinated by the language laboratory we had put in to help missionaries gain fluency in various languages. But then the shock came. I told them how we taught these new missionaries to adjust to Asian cultures, pointing out that the very Westernized and modern city of Singapore forms an ideal bridge between life in the West and their new life in Asia.

'That's ridiculous!' exclaimed one lady. 'Why should we adjust to the way they do things out here? I'm not going to become like a foreigner! If they want to be friends with us, they can learn to do things our way.'

I tried to explain that we were actually living in *their* country and it was up to us to fit in with Asian patterns of behaviour. Otherwise we become a little foreign island, isolated by the streams of life all around us. But the ladies felt that this would threaten their very identity.

Many Jews, Pakistanis and others feel the same in Britain. They feel safe when they can speak their own language, eat their own foods, behave in their own traditional ways. The wider British world around them is very threatening. As far as possible, therefore, they shut themselves off and live huddled together in their own communities.

Such a ghetto community lives constantly under the shadow of cultural attack. It fears that its young people will be lost to the wider life of surrounding society. It sees that its moral values are being undermined. Young English people date whom they want and expect finally to marry the person they want – but the Bangladeshi or Pakistani parents' marriage was arranged by the wider family. And now the young peoples' parents expect to choose whom their children should marry. Asian parents expect immediate obedience from their children, but British society does not encourage it. Sex-ridden and violent films, bad language, alcoholic drink, loud and immodest behaviour – the trends of British life seem dangerous to the rather conservative newcomer.

And we can imagine the family reactions if one of them is converted to the Christian faith. It is seen not just as a religious choice but as a wilful rejection of the old community and of the family. It threatens the identity of them all. No wonder Christian converts may be severely opposed.

The chameleon mentality

'When in Rome, do as the Romans do.' Some immigrants feel it is best to become as much like those around them as possible. If in Britain, then become like the British – dress like them, eat British food, speak English, learn to enjoy British sports and music. Outwardly they become quite British. But inevitably there still remains deep within them something of their cultural background. What we learn as small children never entirely leaves us. And so the culture persists – family attitudes, sense of humour, ways of talking, moral values.

Of course, the culture of the second and third generation of such immigrants may well be totally British. They may not think of themselves at all as foreign, and may have little interest in their family's roots. At least forty per cent of people from ethnic minority groups have been born here. But if they are not accepted as being British they are landed with a real problem of cultural identity. They have not 'adopted' a British lifestyle and outlook on life; they have grown up totally British.

I was talking with the young daughter of a Jewish family. The parents had long since shrugged off their Jewish background and had become very English. The daughter was going on a school trip to Israel and would have Easter in Jerusalem. 'You'll be excited actually to be in Jerusalem,' I exclaimed; 'you must be looking forward to exploring your Jewish roots.' The girl was very surprised and didn't seem to understand what I was saying. She felt – and was – fully English; her parents' background meant nothing to her.

Families who have adapted in this way may be much more open to the Christian faith than those with the ghetto mentality. Like other young British people the children will probably incline towards irreligious materialism, but are not likely to be more opposed to Jesus Christ than other young people. If presented with a relevant and lively witness they may well be ready to listen and respond. And if their parents have also adopted British culture then they won't face heavy opposition at home.

Religion and culture

'How can you still talk of sending missionaries to other countries? They do such damage, destroying native cultures.' Such criticisms can have a basis of truth, but are not the whole story. Not all missionaries bash their way into other cultures without understanding or sensitivity! And the Christian faith, as we shall see, discerns between that which is good in a culture, and that which is inherently evil.

Although it is not always easy in practice to distinguish between culture and religion, they are two different things. *Culture* is the way people behave, think and relate to each other. *Religion* is the relationship people have with God or with whatever spiritual beings they believe in. The difficulty is, of course, that religion actually affects many aspects of culture. And the reverse is equally true – our culture often determines how we express our religion.

Take music as an obvious example. Culture influences religion and so the church has to adapt to more modern musical tastes – old hymns are gradually replaced by modern songs. But religious and moral values also influence music. Not just the words, but also the nature of the music itself reflects the religious or irreligious worldview of the songwriters. And so comes the question: must a converted punk-lover change his musical tastes? And how far should Christians go in adopting modern music? Religion and culture interact.

The attitude of many white young people to their parents could be summed up as, 'I'm not a child any more; I can make my own decisions.' Although many Asian young people long for the freedom of their white friends they are more likely to say, 'I couldn't do that. My parents wouldn't like it.'

What does the Bible have to say about these attitudes? Must the Christian stand against one of these cultures and cause it to change? Some years ago I was invited to speak at a college of education in Asia. On arrival at the campus I was shown the way by a Chinese student who happened to be passing. He looked a bit surprised when I told him that I was to speak at the Christian Union, so I asked him if he was a Christian. 'No,' he said rather strongly, 'I couldn't be a Christian. I am Chinese – and I believe children should obey their parents.'

Somewhere along the line he had got hold of two wrong ideas. He thought Christianity was a Western religion. And then he thought the Western cultural emphasis on individualism was Christian, even if it led to a lack of respect and obedience towards parents and other older people.

In both these assumptions the Chinese student was wrong – although one can understand why he got these ideas. The Christian faith has Jewish roots and is therefore Middle Eastern in its original character. Jesus and the apostles were all Jews. Christianity *has* been adapted to fit a European context, but it can equally well be applied in any other culture. And the Bible has much to teach us about our attitudes to parents and to older people.

Conversion to Jesus Christ does not mean that we all have to adapt to a European way of life and culture. Many churches are thinking about how to relate the Christian faith to other cultures and are asking such questions as: what good things in a culture can be continued and perfected? What bad things need to be attacked and how can they be replaced by something better? In what ways can our worship and the architecture of our churches be fitted to people of different backgrounds? If an African or Asian reads the Bible, does he see things differently from a European? Does the Christian faith need to be expressed in a different way when we relate to people of other cultural or religious backgrounds?

The Christian and other religions

Demonic deception

'I hate Islam; it's demonic', a former missionary in a Muslim country said to me recently. As he spoke I pictured in my mind some Christian books which have been published with striking pictures of an aggressive Khomeini or of massive demonstrations

by shouting Muslim mobs. I get the impression that some
Christians are so frightened of Islam that they can only kick out
at it in self-defence.

But is it true that non-Christian religions are satanic lies, the
Devil's instruments to deceive people and lead them to
damnation? Satan, the father of lies, has played his part in
inspiring the development of all religious systems which deny
the good news of Jesus Christ and prevent people from
following him. But we have also to say that some truth and
goodness can be found in every faith.

Other religions and truth

Last weekend I was speaking in a church and afterwards
talked with a young man who had studied Islam at university.
He was a keen Christian, but was fascinated by the beauty of
the Qur'an, by the apparent simple piety of Muslim worship
and by Islamic culture and art. 'There is so much that is true
and beautiful in Islam,' he told me. 'Somehow it seems a
shame to encourage people to leave all that and become
Christians.'

So are there elements of truth in other religions? Religion is
like human nature, a great mixture of good and bad, of truth
and error. That is not surprising if we reckon that religion
reflects fallen man's search for God. The underlying question
is to what extent fallen man can know God. To the extent that
he can, his religion will contain elements of truth about the
character of God and about what be requires of us.

What then is man like? Some people have a very negative
view of human nature, reckoning it to be completely depraved
and sinful, incapable of recognizing or living by the truth.
Others react against such pessimism and affirm that man is fundamentally good, but perhaps sometimes a little weak. The
Bible, however, sees that we are created in God's image and
likeness, but that this image is corrupted at every point. So
while there is something of God's nature in us, it is sin that
reigns in us. In practice that means that while we may partially
recognize truth, we cannot actually live in line with it. Paul

makes this point in Romans 2:12–16 and again in Romans 3:10–12, when he writes that although God will only judge people on the basis of the 'light' that has been given them, no one manages to live up to the standards that 'light' reveals to them.

So when people are converted from another religion and become followers of Jesus Christ, they bring with them some truths which can carry into their new Christian life. They will also have lovely aspects of their traditional culture which their new faith will not want to negate. But some of their values and beliefs will need to be purified from demonic influences; others will need to be corrected by biblical teaching. For example, the eastern religious emphasis on meditation and deep spirituality has great value in the Christian life, but the practice of self-emptying will need to be replaced by a positive love for Jesus Christ. The mixture of positive and negative within a culture may also be seen in the close-knit extended families of India. These give great support and security, but may rob the individual of personal freedom.

We have all seen reports on TV which tell us that, after months of fear, the police have caught the brutal rapist or murderer. Then his wife is interviewed on the programme and says, 'It can't be him. He's just not that sort of person. He loves me and our small children – and you should see him with our pet cat.' But the evidence is overwhelming. Bestial crime and loving gentleness fit together into the jigsaw of the man's character. And it is equally true of the people we admire and look up to; they too have clay feet. All of us are an amazing combination of beauty and ugliness. Even our highest and best activities are shot through with sin. For example, our loveliest times of prayer and worship contain mixed motives of pride and selfishness – we worship partly because it makes us feel good, for our own benefit rather than for God's pleasure.

'God is great! God is great! God is great!' shouts a militant crowd of fanatical Muslims. The Christian shudders. It's a little like the crusades of earlier Christian times, though that's all past history. But what about some of our current Christian songs which militantly declare that we are 'marching through the land' with the power of God? And isn't it true that God is great? Surely the Bible clearly agrees with these Muslims about God's greatness. Yes, but! What the Muslim believes about God's greatness is not entirely what the New Testament reveals concerning the glorious might and power of God.

Likewise the Muslim creed strongly affirms, 'There is no god but God', but in Islam the doctrine of the oneness of God means an utter rejection of Jesus as the Son of God. The Trinity, which is basic to everything in the Christian faith, is abhorrent to the Muslim – God is one, not three in one. So the Christian's 'Amen' to the Muslim creed can be only partial. Like all religions Islam is a mixture of truth and error.

Involvement with people of other faiths

We will sometimes find ourselves sharing values with those of other faiths, particularly with Jews and Muslims. It can be difficult to know how far to identify with them in social action, whether local or national, and in campaigns over certain moral issues. Often our concerns will be the same as theirs and we can happily participate in action to combat, say, racial attacks. We cannot, however, go so far as to participate in the worship of other religions. The Bible is clear that God alone is to be worshipped and that our worship of him is acceptable only when offered through Christ.

Christian witness

Dialogue

Everyone uses the word dialogue these days, but sometimes we do not really think what it means. It has a double meaning. Firstly, dialogue is distinguished from monologue. The Christian should not preach at others without listening to them. There are good and true things in non-Christian people and faiths, and we need to hear these as they may provide bridges for the gospel. We also need to be aware of the other

person's thoughts and feelings, or our witness will be irrele-
vant. It is also a basic mark of respect for others to listen to,
and discuss with them rather than just preach at them.

Secondly, dialogue is sometimes wrongly used to imply
that *all* we do is listen to the others and learn from them, but
do not aim to bring them to faith in Jesus Christ. If we look at
the New Testament the word dialogue is closely linked to a
witness that proclaims the message of Jesus Christ and desires
that people be converted. So in Acts 17:2 Paul 'dialogued'
(RSV translates it as 'argued') with the people in the synagogue and 17:3 shows that he tried to prove the necessity of
the cross and resurrection. He proclaimed Jesus to be the
Messiah, with the result that some were persuaded and turned
to Jesus. There was also fierce opposition and uproar (17:5) –
how different from some so-called dialogue sessions today!

In true dialogue we will discuss and listen, but our aim will
always be to argue the case for the good news of Jesus Christ.
We will believe that the best possible thing that could happen
to those we talk with is that they should be converted and find
salvation and new life in Christ.

Life and word

In the Old Testament, Israel was called to witness to the surrounding Gentile nations by her life as the people of God. Not
only the individual Jew, but also the whole community together would show God's reality, glory and holiness by their
worship, obedience to God's law and their relationships together. The idea was that Israel's life would then attract the people
of other nations to Jerusalem to worship the God of Israel.

In the New Testament, Jesus sent his disciples out to preach
(Mark 3:13). Although the church would still attract people in
by its life of holiness, love and worship, now it was also to go
out to the world to proclaim verbally the good news of Jesus
Christ.

We witness by life and by word. We attract people in and
we move out into all the world. Our witness to people of all
backgrounds and religious faiths has this double character.

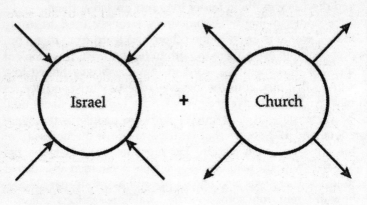

Old Testament   **New Testament**

Israel   +   Church

WITNESS OF LIFE   **WITNESS OF WORD**

Discussion starters

1. 'Britain for the British!' How do you feel about this statement, and why?
2. How do ethnic minorities react to being different from the majority around them? How can we best help them?
3. What problems do the children and grandchildren of immigrant families face as they grow up in their own country of Britain?
4. What should our attitude be to other religions and their followers?
5. How do we recognize what is true in other religions and what is false?
6. 'Life and word' – how do these two relate to each other in our witness?
7. How would you have replied to the student of Islam who said, 'Somehow it seems a shame to encourage people to leave all that and become Christians'?

2

What's so special about Christianity?

If we are to present the Christian gospel effectively to followers of other faiths, it is essential that we live in tolerant and loving peace with them. It is also vital that we hold fast to the uniqueness of Jesus Christ as the one true saviour and Lord, the revealer of God the Father.

The suffering servant

We have already noted that we believe in a God of power. Egyptian magicians could work many miracles in the name of their gods, but Moses outdid them through the power of Yahweh. The Baal gods of nature claimed control over fire and lightning, but only Elijah on Mount Carmel, by calling on the power of the God of Israel, could produce the fire which devoured his sacrifice.

So also Jesus showed his own power over the wind and waves, over demonic powers, over sickness, over sin and over death.

The power of the God of the Bible is greater than that of all other gods or spiritual beings. But the way in which he chooses to display it is unique.

'God would never allow one of his prophets to suffer and die,' a Muslim once said to me. 'How can you believe in a crucified man and say he is God?' Paradoxically, the victory symbol of Christianity is the cross, apparently the place of humiliation and defeat. Yet it was the crucifixion that Jesus called 'My hour'; it was by being lifted up on the cross that he would draw all people to himself (John 12:32). No wonder the early Christians found people often rejected their message! They soon discovered that the truth of a crucified Lord and saviour was 'a stumbling block to Jews and foolishness to Gentiles' (1 Corinthians 1:23).

In one of his books Bishop Cragg emphasizes that this is a basic difference between Islam and Christianity. Both Jesus and Muhammad had few followers at first and in both cases it seemed that their mission was doomed to failure. Muhammad saw that a move from his native Mecca to nearby Medina would enable him both to escape severe persecution and gain power. He became the ruler there, then by military power defeated the people of Mecca and was accepted as both prophet and state leader. Jesus resisted the satanic temptation to take for himself 'all the kingdoms of the world and their splendour' (Matthew 4:8). Although legions of angels stood at his disposal for his defence, he refused to use his power. Jesus accepted the path of weakness and humiliation which took him to the cross. It is only through the suffering servant, Jesus, that God has shown the depth of his love for mankind. This paradox of glory through suffering service and humble self-sacrifice is unique to Christianity and sharply contrary to the natural instincts of us all.

Salvation

The Buddhist gathers merit to improve his chances of escaping the constant repetition of endless reincarnations, in order to be released into the ultimate great void. The Hindu also seeks to escape endless rebirth by his deep devotion, asceticism, good deeds or by losing his self-awareness and sinking like a drop of water into Brahman, the great non-personal Absolute. Neither the Buddhist nor the Hindu has any assured hope of salvation – even as they understand it.

The Muslim tries to follow the revealed will of God and looks forward to the day of judgement when the great heavenly scales will weigh his sins on the one side and his good works on the other. Then it is hoped that the all-merciful God will open the door to paradise, but one can never be sure of God's final decision, although he does normally show mercy on those who do good. But the Bible makes it clear that God has sent his own son Jesus Christ to take upon himself the sin of us all, so that the barrier between God and us has been torn down. Through the sacrificial death of Jesus we know that God's holiness is satisfied, man's sin paid for and the gate to eternal life opened for those who will accept for themselves what Jesus has done for us.

Because of God's saving work in Christ, death has lost its bitter sting. Even though death should be 'untimely', or come suddenly through sickness or accident, we have the confidence of eternal life with the Lord we love. And this eternal life begins here on earth in a new relationship of love with God, through Jesus Christ.

New life in the Spirit

On his deathbed the Buddha told his disciples to work out their own salvation with diligence. The Buddhist believes that each person must therefore strive with all his might to follow the patterns of life established by the teaching of the Buddha.

Muslims see the prophet Muhammad as something of a signpost, pointing out to us the will of God. Now that he has done this and revealed the purpose of Allah, it is up to us to follow God's will by our own efforts. We have free will and can do either good or evil – that is our choice. It is all over to us.

Christians see things very differently. Before he died Jesus promised his disciples that he would not leave them without a comforter. The Holy Spirit would stand alongside them and actually come to live in them. He would direct their minds so that they could know and understand God's revelation of himself. He would work in them to make them increasingly like God, conforming them to the image of Christ.

It is the purpose of God that we should be as righteous and holy as he is himself. So in Galatians 5 we have a list of some of the characteristics of God, which the Holy Spirit is working to develop in us. The New Testament also speaks of the gifts of the Spirit which are given to the church to build it up and display God's glory.

Each Christian is called to play his or her part in the life and ministry of the church, and each is seen to be a temple of the Holy Spirit. There is really no understanding in other faiths which parallels the person and work of the Holy Spirit.

Election, grace and love

We often think that it is we who chose to become Christians and to follow the Lord. The Bible reminds us that the choice was not actually ours – we did not choose God; he chose us! In Mark 3:13 it is recorded that Jesus 'called to him those he wanted'. He chose twelve quite ordinary men to be his disciples, and a number of quite ordinary women were among his closest friends and helpers (Luke 8:2-3).

In all other religions God's favours have to be earned, but the New Testament declares a different way. God chooses totally unworthy sinners, ordinary people, to become his followers and the recipients of his love. This is made possible by the work of Jesus Christ for us. God's grace is unique.

The church

'The next week is going to be very tedious,' said the businessman to his fellow passenger on the plane. 'I am having a week at our factory and I know what lies before me – a five-star hotel all on my own for dinner, the night and breakfast; then the days will be spent discussing money and tins of food before going back again to my hotel room on my own.'

The businessman's companion felt very differently. He looked forward to arriving at his destination, for he would be met by fellow Christians and entertained by them throughout his visit. He belonged to the worldwide Christian family and often experienced the joy of being welcomed by Christian brothers and sisters wherever he went.

The reality of this Spirit-given Christian love surpasses anything found outside the Christian church. Of course there can be a considerable sense of community in all sorts of clubs and groups. Islam strongly emphasizes the *Umma*, the community of the people of Islam. The Muslim's sense of community is heightened by the five times of daily prayer when Muslims all over the world face Mecca together and go through the same prayer ritual in the same Arabic language. Likewise the annual pilgrimage to Mecca adds to the feeling of Islamic oneness as hundreds of thousands of men from all over the world go through the pilgrimage activities together. There is a very real sense of belonging together as fellow Muslims, but the fundamental Christian character of love is missing. Jesus asks of his disciples a love which breaks through barriers of race, culture, class and gender.

Revelation

God is so great that it is impossible for mere man to understand his nature or get to know him in a personal relationship unless God himself takes the initiative. It is therefore vital to discern whether our creed is given by a God who reveals himself or whether it is no more than the expression of human groping after truth. A religion built on the latter may help its followers to climb a few rungs up the ladder, but will never enable him to find God himself.

The Bible

Christianity is not unique in claiming that its holy book is a divine revelation. The Christian faith has grown out of an Old Testament and Jewish root, so we are not surprised to find that Judaism also believes clearly that God has spoken to man in the Jewish Scriptures which we call the Old Testament. Jews affirm that God not only reveals his purposes, but also much of his person and nature, in the Bible. Jewish belief with regard to Scripture closely relates to the Christian understanding.

Islam emerged in Arabia several hundred years after the death of Christ and clearly reflects both Jewish and Christian influences. Islam too is a 'religion of the book'. As a great Muslim writer, Ibn Khaldun, wrote of the Qur'an, 'It is the greatest, noblest and clearest miracle . . . a miracle which is identical with the revelation.' The Muslim believes that God himself wrote the Qur'an on a tablet in heaven before the foundation of the world, so it is in a unique way the word of God – it contains the very words of God. As we shall see, the Christian believes that the Bible too is the word of God, but in a different way. Christians believe that God inspired men who then wrote according to the perfect will of God. But both the Christian and the Muslim declare that God has revealed his purposes in his written word.

The Hindu concept of revelation is much more difficult to grasp. Hindus also have sacred scriptures. The Hindu word *sruti* closely relates to our words revelation or inspiration. But as Hinduism does not always have a clear doctrine of a personal God, it is not altogether easy to define who it is that inspires the Hindu scriptures. In spite of the fact that their holy writings are believed to come by inspiration from above, there is also a sense in which they become sacred because of their extreme antiquity. The origins of the early Hindu writings are wreathed in the mists of pre-history. It is also difficult to define just what they reveal – certainly great truths and ideas, but one cannot really say that they declare either the purposes or the nature of God.

Without doubt, there is no holy book with which the form and content of the Bible may be compared. Its character differs totally from both the Hindu scriptures and the Qur'an. Its aim is also quite distinct. In the Bible God not only reveals his will and doctrinal truths, he also shows us his nature and person, so that we can relate personally to him.

The living word

In the Christian faith God reveals himself supremely in the person of Jesus Christ. Jesus himself claimed that, 'Anyone who has seen me has seen the Father' (John 14:9). In Hinduism, Krishna and other incarnations of the god Vishnu are normally considered to be a part of the god come down to earth. They are not generally thought to be the *fullness* of Vishnu or any other deity, only a part. But of Jesus we are told, 'God was pleased to have all his fulness dwell in him' (Colossians 1:19).

Jesus claimed to be the unique way to God as well as being truth and life personified. In John 14:6 he boldly stated that nobody can come to God the Father except through him. Later, after the resurrection, the apostle Peter likewise boldly preached that, 'Salvation is found in no-one else, for there is no other name under heaven given to men by which we must be saved' (Acts 4:12). There is considerable debate today among Christians as to whether God may apply the saving work of Christ in the cross and resurrection to some people in other faiths. Whatever answer we may come to in this question, we still maintain the uniqueness of Jesus Christ as the perfect revelation of God the Father and the only saviour.

The Bible makes it clear that people cannot be saved through other gods or religions. As the faithful of the Old Testament were saved before Jesus had died, so perhaps God may graciously apply the saving work of Christ to the few followers of other religions who sincerely repent of their sin and humbly trust in God's unmerited grace for their salvation. However, the clear biblical teaching is that we are saved by specific faith in Jesus Christ who died and rose for us.

God

Our understanding of what God is like will fashion the whole character of our faith.

Try explaining to a Muslim that Jesus died on the cross for our sins and you will be asked, 'Why did God need to punish sins?' Muslims point out that as human parents we can forgive our naughty children without necessarily having to punish them every time. If *we* can forgive without punishing surely the omnipotent God can do so! The Muslim places little emphasis on the holy purity of God and therefore cannot understand the sort of problem the apostle Paul faced when he asked how God could remain righteous and yet also justify the sinner. The Qur'an does just mention the holiness of God, but this is not the main thrust of its teaching about Allah. In contrast, one glance at the word 'holy' in a concordance will show that righteous holiness is a fundamental element in biblical teaching about God. The Muslim finds Christian teaching about the way of salvation very hard to grasp.

'You call yourself a Christian and yet you . . .' is a common accusation which non-Christians in Europe use to attack believers in Christ. They assume that someone who claims to be a Christian ought to live a good life. Where did they get that idea from? From the whole tradition of Christian influence in our culture. The Bible teaches again and again that true worship of the holy God needs to be matched by holy living – we are to be holy as he is holy. In contrast, as a follower of New Age or modern Western paganism you can be 'spiritual' without necessarily being morally holy.

We have already noted that the Bible shows God to be patiently loving and full of grace. These same characteristics should be mirrored in the lives of his followers. So the New Testament constantly repeats the exhortation to be patient, loving and gracious, not only to lovable people and those who can return the honour, but also to the disadvantaged and those who sin against us. We are to be like our God.

When we look at Buddhism we shall see that the Buddha stressed a dispassionate separation from the world and its desires. Statues and pictures of the Buddha often show him with a smile on his face – the cool smile of non-involvement, not the warm smile of humour or happiness. There is therefore a tendency among Buddhists to become very gentle, quiet people who seek to avoid emotional involvement in the world. The God of the Bible is quite different. He loves with a passionate, warm-hearted concern. Sin angers and pains him. Goodness and faith cause him to rejoice. He actively involves himself in the movements of history, in the concerns of the world and of each one of us.

In Hinduism, Brahman, the absolute ultimate reality, is not personal. Brahman does not therefore engage in personal relationships. The biblical God, however, has within himself an intimate communication of love – the Father with the Son, the Son with the Spirit, each with the others. The Christian therefore wants to affirm personal existence, character and personality. We affirm the goodness of human relationships, and of loving personal communication. (See M. Goldsmith, *Jesus and his Relationships*, Paternoster, 2000.

Discussion starters

1. 'What's so special about Christianity?' How would you answer someone who asked you this?

2. What do you understand by the word 'salvation'?

3. What difference does the lordship of Christ make to your everyday life?

4. The church is the family of God's children and he is our Father. What could you do to enjoy this fact more and also to encourage others in this?

5. What is grace? How important is it to the Christian faith? What does grace show us about the character of God and the nature of our relationship with him? (You may find it helpful to read Romans 8:1-4.)

6. Share together how God has shown his loving grace towards you and what difference this has made in your life.

7. How would you answer someone who said, 'All religions lead to God; Christianity is just one way of getting there'?

PART I

The major world religions

3

Judaism

What is a Jew?

If you drive through the Stamford Hill area of London, or Gateshead in the north, it is easy to pick out Jewish people. The men are readily identified by their long black coats, black hats, side curls and long beards. But if you have many Jewish friends or colleagues you will know some who have blonde or auburn hair, blue eyes, and who just do not fit the common stereotype. If you spend a holiday in Israel or the eastern Mediterranean you may find it difficult to distinguish Greeks or Arabs from Jews if they're all in modern, Western clothes and you can't decipher which languages are being spoken.

Does the term 'Jew' describe appearance, religion, political stance or race? This is Judaism's big question: it has been debated down the ages and still is today in the Knesset (the Israeli parliament) and in the Israeli law courts.

A Jew by birth

When the eleventh-century Christian crusaders wanted money to finance their expeditions against the Muslim 'infidels' living in Jerusalem and the Holy Land, they attacked Jewish towns and villages in Europe. On the grounds that the Jews had crucified Jesus over ten centuries before, they killed many of the men, stole their property and raped their women. These devastated communities ensured that the children born of those savage attacks would be accepted as Jewish, by making it the practice to consider anyone born of a Jewish mother as Jewish. This is the legal code today.

A Jew by conversion

Among more liberal Jews, Gentiles who convert to Judaism are accepted as Jews. They are expected to do a course of study in the teachings and practices of Judaism. Women converts are required to have a ritual bath, a *mikveh*. Sometimes this is required of the men too. Alternatively, they may have their finger pricked to shed blood, instead of circumcision. Strictly orthodox Jews strongly dissuade Gentiles from being converted; they encourage them to be righteous Gentiles.

The confusion over who may be accepted as a Jew, and on what grounds, was highlighted in the 1980s by the controversy in Israel over the Felasha Jews – brought to Israel to escape the famine in Ethiopia. Their long-term history was shrouded in mystery and their claim to 2,000 years of Jewish ancestry could not be verified. Because it was possible that their ancestors could have been converts to Judaism, rather than the descendants of Jews, the Israeli Orthodox insisted that they must be immersed in a ritual bath – a *mikveh* – before they could be fully accepted as Jews and Israeli citizens.

A Jew who changes religion?

Another problem arises if Jewish people come to believe in Jesus or convert to any other religion. If a Jewish person has no faith at all and calls himself an atheist, he can still be a Jew and an Israeli citizen. If he is baptized as a Christian and wishes to become an Israeli citizen, he will be considered a non-Jew and fail to gain citizenship. Among Jewish communities in Britain, Europe and the USA, where the question of citizenship does not arise, a convert will nevertheless be regarded as a traitor to the Jewish community and therefore no longer a Jew. In the past some families would hold a funeral service for a member who had become a Christian believer. Even today some might put an obituary notice in the *Jewish Chronicle*.

So the definition of a Jew, which is accepted by most Jews, is that he or she is a person born of a Jewish mother and has not changed his or her religion.

Beliefs

For the Jewish people the Scriptures are the Law, the Prophets and the Writings, known to them as the Tenach and to Christians as the Old Testament. They give special prominence to the Law, the first five books of the Bible.

In their desire not to break any of the law of Moses, strictly religious Jews have fenced it round with extra regulations and interpretations. From the earliest times of Israel's faith there grew up an oral tradition, explaining and defining the written law clearly. This was known as the Oral Torah. In about AD 200 – or, as the Jews would say, 200 CE (common Era) – when they began to fear there was too much to be remembered orally, it was written down and called the Mishnah. Commentaries or Gemara were then written on the Mishnah. The two, Mishnah and Gemara, were combined about 500 CE and became known as the Talmud. So Jewish scholars today don't just study the Torah – the Law of Moses – or the Tenach, but the Talmud as well. The novels of Chaim Potok give a good insight into the ultra-orthodox community of New York and the importance to them of Talmudic studies.

The beliefs of Jewish people are based not just on the law of Moses or on the Tenach, but also on the views of their rabbis down the centuries.

As Christians, we are indebted to the Jewish Scriptures for our knowledge of God who created the world and made man in his own image. We share a belief in the failure of mankind to obey a holy and righteous God and in our consequent need of atonement for sin. Since the destruction of the Temple in AD 70 most Jews have believed that atonement is not gained by the blood of sacrifices, but through prayer, repentance and the performance of good deeds. This means they do not have the Christian's individual assurance of sins forgiven.

The Jews believe in one God, creator and sovereign Lord and often assume that Christians believe in three gods. Maimonides, a thirteenth-century rabbi, drew up thirteen principles of Jewish belief in order to preserve Judaism against the attack of Christian doctrine. This is the nearest there is to a Jewish creed, but it does not encompass the fullness of Judaism. To the Jew the way in which one lives is more important than belief. But because of Christian opposition and persecution Maimonides stressed the following, countering the Christian doctrine of the Trinity, belief in the deity of Jesus, and the gospel which proclaims salvation apart from keeping the law:

'God is unity, He alone is our God . . . to Him alone is it right to pray . . . He is the first and the last.'

'Moses was the chief of the prophets, both of those that preceded and of those that followed him.'

'This Law will not be changed, and there will never be any other law.'

It is not usually helpful for Christians to argue with Jewish friends about the deity of Jesus Christ. It is better to encourage them to read the New Testament where they will see for themselves the Jewishness of Jesus and his disciples. It will help them to understand how, despite their monotheistic background, the disciples came to accept Jesus as their Messiah and Lord, and how Thomas came to say to Jesus, 'My Lord and my God'.

Most Jews are no longer looking for a personal Messiah as Maimonides was, so it does not always mean much to modern Jews to speak about Jesus as the Messiah. They have been disappointed in their past expectations and are now looking forward to a 'Messianic Age', a time when truth, justice and peace will be established throughout the world. If they are willing to read about Jesus, Matthew's Gospel is the one they may find most helpful. They may also be willing to look again at the messianic prophecies in their Scriptures. Many Jews have never, for example, read passages like Isaiah 52 and 53 which speak of the suffering of the Messiah.

Judaism's cultural groups

There are two main groups of Jews, the Sephardim and the Ashkenazim.

The Sephardim

This group is descended from Spanish and Portuguese Jews who were driven out of Spain by the Inquisition in 1492. Some came to countries like Britain and America but many went to North Africa and the Middle East and influenced Jews there. They are the smaller group in Britain and the USA but they have the oldest synagogues.

The Ashkenazim

This group originated in Germany and Eastern Europe and large numbers now live in Britain, North and South America and Australia. Their cultural heritage is associated with the language of Yiddish – a mixture of German and Hebrew.

Judaism's religious groups

As Jewish people vary in appearance, depending on where their ancestors came from, so they vary in their religious practices. Some have given up attendance at synagogue altogether, celebrate no festivals in their homes and are fully assimilated into the culture of their host country. But even among these many would still work in Jewish businesses, have many Jewish friends and a great love for Israel.

In Britain, the USA and other Western countries where there are large Jewish communities, there are four basic religious groups.

Ultra-orthodox Judaism

This is the most religious of the four groups, and regards itself
as the true Judaism. It is ultra-orthodox in its strict adherence
to the commandments given in the Torah, applying them to
every aspect of life. One of their organizations, the Lubavitch
Foundation, is concerned to win all Jews back to the core of
their religion – obedience to the law. Members of the organization visit Jewish homes to encourage families to follow strict
religious practices.

The largest group of ultra-orthodox Jews in Israel live in the
Mea Sherim area of Jerusalem. They tend not to be concerned
with politics and the economy, but a few have entered the
Israeli parliament in order to exert as strong an influence as
they can to prevent Israel becoming a secular nation. In their
area of Jerusalem they do not allow any form of motor trans-
port on the Sabbath, and they would like to bring in legislation
to ban all work and travel on the Sabbath throughout Israel.

In England ultra-orthodox Jews are well established in the
Stamford Hill area of London and in Gateshead. The men and
even the small boys dress very conservatively in black clothes
typical of eighteenth-century Poland, and wear their hair long
in side locks. When older they have beards too. The women
wear long dresses with long sleeves. After an ultra-orthodox
woman is married her head will be shaved and she will wear
a wig in public. The men devote themselves to the study of the
Torah in schools and colleges know as Yeshivas. Their wives
attend to all the domestic requirements of a strictly religious
Jewish household besides looking after the many children that
an ultra-orthodox family would usually have.

Orthodox Judaism

Towards the end of the nineteenth century large numbers of
Jews began to leave Eastern Europe for America and with this
uprooting came a more open attitude to the culture of the
modern West. Orthodox Jews still centre their lives on the
commands of the Torah but are prepared to adapt their

religious practices to the demands of the culture in which they live – so long as the two do not conflict. These Jews therefore dress in a way appropriate to their resident country but with the addition in some cases of prayer caps. They observe the religious laws concerning their homes, food and the Sabbath. They attend synagogue regularly and celebrate all the Jewish festivals. Some men train in the Jewish law and become rabbis but many are involved in normal occupations. The children will, if possible, attend Jewish schools.

In their synagogues the women usually sit separately, either in a gallery or at the back. The services are still mainly in Hebrew and only men take part in the reading. They live close to their synagogue in order to be able to walk there. In Britain different groups exist, like the United Synagogues and the Federation of Synagogues, and practices are more traditional in some than others.

Reform Judaism

The Reform movement began in Germany at the beginning of the eighteenth century. It followed the establishment, in nearly all the European countries conquered by Napoleon, of the principle of religious toleration. Many Jews felt it was in keeping with this new spirit of openness to adapt their practices as much as possible to the outside world.

The most obvious change to the outsider was the way in which synagogue services were altered to become more like church services, including sermons and organ playing. Men and women sit together in the Reform synagogue and girls of twelve are able to have a religious coming-of-age service – bat mitzvah – to correspond to the bar mitzvah service held for Jewish boys. Part of the service may be in Hebrew but in Britain and the USA much of the service is in English. The prayer books have a complete translation of the Hebrew. Jews of the Reform movement are happy to drive to synagogue on the Sabbath, if necessary.

At home they celebrate the traditional festivals and make the Sabbath a special day, but are not concerned with all the

minutiae of Jewish law. They switch on electric lights, the TV
and the cooker on the Sabbath and so don't feel the necessity
to install time switches, as the more orthodox Jews do. When
on holiday, if they cannot afford or obtain acceptable Jewish
food some will eat whatever is available.

Liberal and Progressive Judaism

The emergence of a liberal Judaism was the natural result of
the reformed Judaism of the nineteenth century. The
Enlightenment affected Judaism as much as Christianity, in
that authority and tradition were both called into question, as
was the extent of the relevance of the ancient Scriptures to the
modern world.

Today, Liberal and Progressive Jews do not have to observe
the Jewish laws strictly, as they consider them to have been
given to Israel when it was a rural, nomadic people and are
therefore not appropriate in all their details for the world of
the twentieth century. They concentrate on the ethical teaching
of the Torah rather than on the ritual law.

Their synagogues are similar to modern Christian churches.
Men and women sit together. There might even be a woman
rabbi. In Britain, Rabbi Julia Neuberger became well known
through her radio and television broadcasts. The service of a
Liberal or Progressive Synagogue is in English or the local language, not Hebrew.

A liberal Jew will attend synagogue, celebrate festivals and
enjoy the Sabbath in much the same way as a Christian will
attend church, celebrate Christmas and Easter, and use
Sunday.

In addition to these four religious groupings, many Jews
have been assimilated into their local culture and practices.
For example, the grandparents of a family may attend synagogue regularly but the parents might go only once a year on
the day of Atonement and the grandchildren may never go.
The parents might have regular holidays in Israel especially at
Passover and the children may spend a year on a Kibbutz, but
in some cases the only festival they celebrate is Christmas! The

first task one Jewish student was asked to do on coming home from university in December was to put up the Christmas tree and the lights before he went out to visit his friends!

Many people of Jewish origin may, in fact, no longer consider themselves Jewish. An elderly lady with a distinct German accent and quite typical Jewish looks, living in Golders Green, said to me, 'No one would ever know I was born Jewish. As soon as I came to England after the war I had my children christened and became British.'

With the greater affluence of the post-war years in Britain the birth rate dropped among all groups of Jews, except the ultra-orthodox. Many Jews also moved outside traditional Jewish areas and were assimilated into the local community. In 1970 there were over 400,000 Jews in Britain with Jewish affiliation; but by 2001 there were only 300,000.

Bearing in mind these different traditions we will go on to look at the way Judaism affects the day-to-day life of its people. The practices referred to will be those generally observed by orthodox Jews, though others will also be noted.

The Synagogue

It would be more accurate to compare the synagogue to a community centre rather than to a Christian church. In Old Testament times the centre of Jewish worship was the Temple in Jerusalem. When that was destroyed by the Babylonians in 587 BC the Jews were taken away from their land into exile. They began to meet together in small groups to study their law.

These 'gatherings together' were the original synagogues (Greek: *sun* together, *ago* to bring). Later, on their return to the land of Israel, the Jews were allowed to rebuild the Temple. So in the time of Christ the Temple was the centre of worship and the synagogues were places where the Jewish scriptures were read and the law was taught to the people.

In AD 70 the Romans destroyed the Temple; it has never been rebuilt. All that remains is the western supporting wall of the Temple area, known as the Wailing Wall. Today many Jews go there to pray or to celebrate their sons' religious coming of age at thirteen.

Now there is no central place of worship for Jews, but there are many synagogues all over the world. These are still primarily places of meeting together to hear the Scriptures read and study the law. Prayers are said too, but worship is not the prime purpose of meeting in the synagogue. Christians attending a synagogue are often surprised to see a man praying one moment and then walking over to a friend and talking to him while the service continues. The women, especially when sitting separately, often chat to one another and even attract their husband's attention to come and speak to them.

All synagogues have a raised platform in the front from which the law and the prophets are read and the service is led. In a reformed or progressive synagogue the sermon will also be preached from there. Set readings of the law are prescribed for each service.

A synagogue cannot be formed or a service held unless there is a quorum of ten men – a *minyan*. No number of women will make up for the absence of one man!

Hymns are not sung in orthodox synagogues nor will there be any choir or musical instruments.

In the synagogue complex there are also rooms for teaching children, facilities for Hebrew classes, a library, a hall for social functions and recreation, and sometimes even a gymnasium.

The home

While much of Jewish social life centres on the synagogue, much of Jewish religious life centres on the home. Since there is no demand for a woman to attend synagogue or study the law, Christians might feel that the Jewish woman is left out of the religious aspects of Judaism. Yet, though she is given no religious duties which occur at fixed times because she may have a baby to feed or a festival meal to prepare, it is the woman's job to keep a good Jewish home and teach the children to pray and know the law.

Dietary Laws (Kashrut)

A Jewish wife is expected to keep a kosher household, that is to observe strictly all the food laws. Forbidden foods include pork, rabbit and shellfish, and such things as suet or gelatine (see Leviticus 11 and Deuteronomy 14). The meat must be slaughtered in the orthodox way. Milk, or milk products and meat cannot be eaten at the same time. This is because of the biblical command not to boil a kid in its mother's milk (see Exodus 23:19, 34:26; Deuteronomy 14:21). Some will not eat milk within an hour of meat, others wait for three hours. This means that a meat dinner cannot be followed by cheese and biscuits, or milk or cream in coffee. Dishes like lasagne, which contain meat and milk, are definitely not kosher! In an orthodox home separate sets of crockery and tea towels will be used for milk and meat dishes. If you wish to offer hospitality to Jewish friends, it is wise to ask beforehand what they would like to eat. Some orthodox Jews will prefer only to have a drink of milkless tea out of a glass. Others will be happy to have a salmon or chicken salad. Many young Jewish people from non-observant families will eat anything, even pork sausages and bacon!

Sabbath

In a Jewish home preparations for the Sabbath begin on Friday. The wife needs to have all the special food prepared during the day and to be ready at sunset to light the Sabbath candles. Then the family sit down to a celebration meal. If as a church you are planning a neighbourhood visit it is best not to disturb Jewish homes on a Friday evening.

On the Saturday morning the whole family, if possible, will go to synagogue. The devout Jew may study the Scriptures in the afternoon. In many homes the children will be allowed to play family games in the afternoon or may visit relatives who live nearby. The reason for abstaining from normal tasks is to give a sense of timelessness, a brief foretaste of the age to come. At the end of the day they recite blessings over a cup of wine and a box of sweet spices. The fragrance of the spices is symbolic of the sweetness of the Sabbath that they hope will be carried into the next week.

Mezuzah and Phylacteries

On the front door of the house and on all the doorposts inside, except the bathroom, is fixed the mezuzah, a small oblong box. Inside are the words that form the core of the Jewish faith, the *shema*: 'Hear, O Israel: the Lord our God, the Lord is One. You shall love the Lord your God with all your heart and with all your soul and with all your strength' (Deuteronomy 6:4-5). They write this out in response to Deuteronomy 6:9 where the Israelites were instructed to write the commandments of the Lord on the doorposts of the house. The Lubavitch Foundation are willing to check mezuzoth and change any that are not valid – they may, for instance, have been painted over or the parchment inside may be lost, torn or illegible.

Orthodox Jewish men are expected to pray each day at home as well as attend synagogue when possible. They tie phylacteries on their arms and foreheads before praying. These are small leather boxes with long leather straps, containing quotations from the law. This they do in accordance with Deuteronomy 6:8; it is a visible symbol that they keep the law close to their heads and their hearts.

The festivals

In Jewish religious life the sacred and the secular are more closely entwined than in the lives of many Christians. The only day in the year when every Jew must attend synagogue is a fast day, the Day of Atonement. For the main festivals there are special services in the synagogues but all the customary celebrations take place in the home. We have already looked at the Sabbath as it is celebrated in the home. It is the most important Jewish festival, commemorating creation.

Jewish people follow an ancient calendar based on the lunar month, and the date of each festival varies each year. The origin of these festivals is to be found in the Jewish Scriptures – our Old Testament.

New Year: Rosh Hoshanah

New Year is celebrated in September or October. It is the time to celebrate God's creation of the world and all Jews send cards to each other. Apples dipped in honey are a speciality at this festival, linked with wishing each other 'a good and sweet year'. The orthodox will take ten days' holiday for a time of self-examination and repentance.

Day of Atonement: Yom Kippur

After ten days will come the day when no work is done and all Jews except small children, pregnant women, and the sick, fast from sunset to sunset. Any Jew who is at all religious attends synagogue on Yom Kippur so the synagogues often need to hire halls or cinemas to accommodate the large numbers. They spend the day praying and confessing their sins. After sunset on the second evening they gather at home for a celebration meal. This day has become memorable in modern history because of Egypt's attack on Israel on the Day of Atonement in 1973. The subsequent war has become known at the Yom Kippur War.

Tabernacles: Sukkot

Five days after Yom Kippur is the feast of tabernacles or booths. In hot climates Jews build temporary shelters of branches in their gardens or on the roofs of their houses and live outdoors for a week. This is a reminder of God's miraculous provision for them when they lived in tents in the wilderness. In Britain they still build shelters in their gardens and, if the weather permits, have parties or special meals out there. This is a time to thank God for material blessings and to look forward to the time of future blessing when the Messiah comes. The Christian harvest festival derives from this Feast of Tabernacles.

Rejoicing in the law: Simchat Torah

During the course of a year the whole of the Torah, the first five books of the Bible, is read in the synagogue. On this festival day the reading is completed with the last portion of Deuteronomy, and begun again with the first verses of Genesis. The service is a very joyful one and the scrolls of the law are carried in procession around the synagogue with singing and dancing.

Festival of Light: Hanukkah

This takes place in December. It commemorates the victory of Judas Maccabeus over the Syrians, and the re-dedication of the temple in Jerusalem in 164 BC. A nine-branched candlestick is lit. On the eight days of the festival a candle is lit each day from the servant candle in the centre. Many Jewish families in Christian countries give presents to each other at this festival because it normally occurs around the time of Christmas.

Purim

This festival takes place in February or March and celebrates the events of the book of Esther. It is a time for parties, often in fancy dress, and for eating special three-cornered pastries called Haman's Pockets.

Passover: Pesach

This festival takes place in March or April and recalls the deliverance of the people of Israel from their slavery in Egypt. A special meal, *seder*, is held in the home. Traditional dishes are eaten, songs are sung and the story of the deliverance from Egypt is recounted. A place at the table is always left vacant for the prophet Elijah, who is expected to come as a herald of the Messianic Age. On the eve of the Passover a thorough search is made in each Jewish home to ensure that no leaven (yeast) has been left anywhere. During this feast unleavened bread is eaten to remind the Jews of 'the bread of affliction' which Jewish slaves ate in Egypt.

Pentecost: Shavuot

Fifty days after Passover, in May or June, the festival of Pentecost is celebrated. It commemorates the giving of the law by God to Moses on Sinai. The ten commandments are read in the synagogue, which is decorated with flowers and plants as this is also the Feast of the First Fruits.

Life

Circumcision

On the eighth day after his birth a Jewish boy is circumcised. This may be done by a doctor in hospital, but orthodox Jews will have it done by a *mohel*, a man trained and approved by the community, at home or in the synagogue. A boy child is named at the circumcision ceremony. A girl is named in the synagogue service the Sabbath after her birth.

Bar mitzvah

The bar mitzvah (son of the commandment) ceremony takes place in the synagogue when a boy of thirteen takes on himself the obligations of the law. He is called to read one of the portions of scripture set for that day. In the reformed synagogues girls of thirteen have a corresponding ceremony called bat mitzvah.

Marriage

This is viewed as a holy covenant. Before the ceremony the
groom signs the marriage document (*ketubbah*) in which he
pledges himself to the bride. During the service the couple
stand under a canopy (*huppah*) representative of their future
home. At the end a glass is broken and seven blessings are
recited. All these events in Jewish families warrant lively celebrations and they often invite their Gentile friends to celebrate
with them. You can show your love for them by rejoicing with
them.

Death

A religious Jew will want to utter the words of the *shema* on his
deathbed. Others present will make a small tear in their
clothes. The funeral will be held if possible within twenty-four
hours of a death. The family spend seven days in mourning at
home, they do no work but just sit (known as sitting *shiva*)
while friends visit them and bring food. Short visits from
Gentile friends will be appreciated too. The mourners' prayer
of praise, *kaddish*, is said at the funeral and daily thereafter in
the synagogue for a month. On the anniversary of the death of
a parent the children light a memorial candle and recite the
kaddish at the end of the synagogue service.

Persecution and the holocaust

No one can understand Jewish people and Judaism today
unless they know their history of persecution. If we read
Jewish Scriptures we will know of their slavery in Egypt, their
exile in Babylon and the beginnings of the Jewish dispersion.
During the time of Christ they were subjugated to the Romans
in Palestine. In AD 70 Jerusalem was destroyed and the story of
the last stand of the Jewish nationalists at Massada is well
known. From then on, Jews were scattered throughout the
world, very few remaining in Palestine.

In the middle ages, as we have already noted, Jews in Europe were attacked, their women raped and their property looted by Christian soldiers in order to finance their crusades against the Muslims. They were made to wear distinctive clothes or symbols to show that they were Jews and were then always on the move – banished from one country after another.

After the Norman conquest of 1066 Jews settled in Britain. But here too they suffered ill-treatment. When in 1144, a boy was found murdered in Norwich the Jews were accused of killing him to use his blood at Passover! A furious mob fell on the Jewish quarter and many Jews were massacred. In 1190 in the city of York 1500 Jews fled for refuge to Clifford's Tower to avoid an angry Christian mob. They were besieged for three days but then, rather than be massacred by the Christians, they took their own lives. Finally, in 1290 all Jews were expelled from Britain. They were not allowed to return until Cromwell's time in 1650.

Many other European countries followed suit in the next two decades, including Italy and France. In 1348 the Jews were accused of poisoning wells and causing the Black Death in Europe and many were massacred. In Spain they enjoyed a golden age under the Muslims but under the Christian rulers they suffered torture and death during the Inquisition. By 1492 all Jews had fled Spain.

In the eighteenth and nineteenth centuries those living in Eastern Europe were forced to live in segregated areas or ghettoes. On Good Friday they had to stay locked in their homes for fear of mobs coming to take revenge on them for the death of Jesus. After 1880 the situation in Russia under the Christian Tsars got worse. Jewish property was burned and whole communities were driven from their homes in what became known as the Russian Pogroms. Many emigrated to England and America. The musical, *Fiddler on the Roof*, is set in this period.

From about 1700 a more enlightened attitude grew in Western Europe. Many Jews settled in France, Germany and Britain and rose to prominent positions, especially in finance and commerce. But in the 1880s strong anti-Semitic movements began again in France and Germany, this time based on the idea of the superiority of the Aryan race. These climaxed in Hitler's 'final solution', when six million Jews died in the concentration camps and gas chambers of the Holocaust.

Is it any wonder that the sign of the cross brings fear even today to Jews? The cross, which is the symbol of God's love for man, has been twisted into a swastika, symbol of man's hatred for the Jew. It can be very hurtful for a Jew to see a Christian wearing a cross as an ornament, maybe on a necklace. Is it surprising that a Jew being baptized brings great sorrow to other Jews as they remember forced baptisms? A Jew who becomes a Christian has gone over to the other side. He is seen as a traitor to his ancestors who died to preserve the Jewish faith under militant attack from 'Christians'. Today many Jews are happily settled in Western countries, but in the back of their minds there is always the fear that the horrors of the Holocaust, which took place in the twentieth century in a Christian country, could happen again.

Israel

With such a history of persecution, the state of Israel is of great importance to Jews today. If persecution should ever break out again they have a refuge, a homeland. This is why many peace-loving, prosperous Jews are willing to fight for Israel. Some Western Jews see the incongruity of their own treatment of the Palestinians who have lived in the land of Israel for centuries. They do not want to persecute them, but they do feel the need to preserve their own small land against attack from their many Arab neighbours.

There have always been a few Jews living in 'the Land'. But at the end of the nineteenth century and during the first half of the twentieth many fled from the persecutions in Russia and Germany and settled in Israel. After the War of Independence in 1948 a Jewish, Hebrew-speaking state was established. Three million Jews from many different countries and backgrounds have emigrated (made *aliyah*) to Israel. The development of the parched land into a modern Western-type state, and the integration of those many different nationalities, has been one of the miracles of the twentieth century. But it has brought its own tensions, not only with the Arabs outside the state and the Palestinians within, but between the Ashkenazi and Sephardi communities, between the ultra-orthodox and the non-religious, between the conservative and the liberal, the militant and the peace-loving. The enormous military budget has caused high inflation and without the financial support for the state from Jews all over the world, especially in the USA, it is doubtful whether the nation could have survived. Today the government still struggles to find solutions to the problems inherent in its diverse community.

Christian witness

Today in the States there are many thousands of Jewish people who believe in Jesus as their Messiah. In Israel and Britain the number is in the hundreds and steadily growing. Most Jewish people who have become believers in Britain have done so not because of direct evangelism from a stranger but through the friendship and witness of a Christian friend. One Jewish schoolboy was ill for a year and a young Christian friend visited him every day after school. When he recovered he went to the friend's youth fellowship, believed in Jesus and is now an evangelist. A Jewish lady whose husband left her worked with a Christian. The Christian's love and concern led her to faith in Jesus. A Jewish man spent a year discussing his inability to believe in God with a Christian friend. Once he believed in God, he said that it was a simple step to believe in Jesus.

Jews have suffered persecution from Christians in the past and they need to know the long-term love and friendship of Christians if they are to be attracted to Jesus. Some will read about Jesus, some will be interested enough to go to Christian meetings or services but not many will do that on their own. A

few even after believing in Jesus may find it very difficult to
enter a church. When they are baptized their families will find
it difficult to understand.

If you wish to help Jewish people to become believers in
Jesus you should check your own attitude. Do you tell anti-
Semitic jokes to make them laugh, or make sweeping general-
izations like 'all Jews are rich', 'all Jews are pushy', and 'all
Jews are racists'? What you are and what you do will be the
first witness to your Jewish colleagues or neighbours. Your
love and your life will earn you the right to speak of what you
believe.

Discussion starters

1. Describe any Jewish people known to you personally – their beliefs, their practices, their attitudes, any distinctive clothing.

2. Where have you met Jewish people? Where is the Jewish community nearest to you? What are its characteristics? Are any other Jewish communities known to members of this group? If so describe them.

3. How much of our Christian faith do we owe to the Jews and share in common with them?

4. What has Christianity to offer Jewish people that cannot be found in Judaism?

5. 'Most modern Jews are no longer looking for a personal Messiah... They have been disappointed in their past expectations and are now looking forward to a 'Messianic Age,' a time when truth, justice and peace will be established throughout the world' (p 32). How do you react to this statement?

6. Why is it important to know what sort of background a Jewish person is from when you are witnessing to them of Jesus?

7. 'While much of Jewish social life centres on the synagogue, much of Jewish religious life centres on the home' (p 41-42). Should the church and the home have a similar role in the Christian faith? Why or why not? What do you think the advantages and the drawbacks are?

8. What do you feel about the persecution of Jews down the centuries? What signs of anti-Semitism do you think there are today in your country, your community or in you?

4

Islam

There are some 800 million Muslims around the world, following the faith of Islam – and about a million of these are in Britain. They have declared Europe to be their primary mission field and aim to convert that continent to Islam. Many are confident that this will be done, and maintain a real sense of power.

What then does it mean to be a Muslim? The word *Islam* means submission, while *Muslim* signifies the one who submits. We have all seen pictures of Muslim men kneeling in prayer with their foreheads to the ground – prostrate as a sign of submission to Allah / God and his Prophet Muhammad.

Muhammad

Born in Mecca around AD 570 of poor trading parents, the young Muhammad grew up surrounded by materialistic paganism. Deeply religious himself, he reacted against such idolatry and self-seeking. In this he was also influenced by some Jews and Christians in the area of Mecca, and would spend whole nights alone in prayer in a cave. One night he had a vision of the Archangel Gabriel coming to him in splendour and telling him, 'You are the messenger of God.' Then he was told to warn the people of Mecca that judgment would come upon them if they did not submit in faith to Allah and to Muhammad his prophet.

At first most people rejected his message and eventually he had to flee to neighbouring Medina where the people had asked him to be their leader. With them he fought and beat the Meccans, so establishing Islam in this central part of Arabia. Having returned in triumph to Mecca he died in AD 632, but his work was carried on by his followers. He was succeeded by four great Caliphs, the last of which was his famous son-in-law, Ali. Through them Islam conquered most of the Middle East, North Africa, Spain and much of France. Eastwards, its armies took Islam as far as India.

In succeeding centuries Muslim traders took their faith to Indonesia and Malaysia, down the east coast of Africa and across the Sahara to West Africa. To the world's amazement this unknown desert religion utterly defeated the great empires of the day – Persia, Rome, Byzantium. And when the Turkish hordes swept into the west from Mongolia, they too converted to Islam.

But there were also defeats. The French King, Charles Martel, drove the Muslims from France at the battle of Tours in AD 732 and the fearful horrors of the Crusades in the eleventh and twelfth centuries caused untold suffering which have still not been forgotten by Muslims. This is why Christians should never use militant words like 'Crusade' when witnessing to Muslims. In more recent times Muslim power was eclipsed by the imperial powers of the West.

In the 1960s the various Muslim lands regained their national independence, while in the 1970s, the oil crisis turned unknown, little desert states into significant world powers. Muslims felt God was now on their side, showing the world that Islam is the one true faith. Since then Islam has been on the march with its militant chant, *Allahu Akbar*, 'God is great'.

Qur'an and Sunna

During his time in Mecca and Medina Muhammad claimed to have received a series of revelations through the archangel Gabriel. These were gathered together to form the Qur'an and are believed by Muslims to be a word-for-word copy of what had been engraved by God on a tablet in heaven before the creation of the world. Emphasis is placed on the illiteracy of Muhammad as evidence that he could not have composed the Qur'an himself. It is written in very beautiful Arabic, particularly the earlier sections.

The Qur'an consists of 114 suras or chapters, all but one of which begins with the title. 'In the name of Allah, the compassionate, the merciful'. The suras are placed in order of length, not chronologically or in any sequence according to their meaning. Most Muslim boys will learn to recite the Qur'an in Arabic by heart and Muslims give it great reverence. It is believed to have almost magical powers and just the act of reciting it brings blessing.

The Christian Bible claims to have been written by a number of men under the inspiration of the Holy Spirit. Its contents are directly related to the context in which it was written. For example, Luke's Gospel bears the character of Luke the Gentile doctor, and relates to the debates of his time. The Qur'an however is said to have no such human participation: God writes, Muhammad is only the passive channel through whom he dictates. While the Christian therefore struggles to understand the Bible in its original context and only then relates it to today's world, the Muslim sees the Qur'an as the timeless words of God to be applied directly to today without any cultural adjustment or criticism. The Muslim has some difficulty in adjusting his religion to different cultural situations, while Christians may sometimes be so culturally flexible that they lose the rock-like assurance of unchanging revelation.

After the death of Muhammad many traditions were recorded of the deeds, words and unspoken thoughts of Muhammad. These were brought together in several collections and are known as the Hadith (traditions). The Hadith contains the Sunna, or example of Muhammad's behaviour and way of life. Although the Sunna of Mohammed is always considered to be secondary to the Holy Qur'an, much of Islam is based on it. Together, the Qur'an and the Sunna form Islamic law.

Beliefs

The Five Pillars of Islam

We have noted that Islam means submission. To what does a Muslim submit when he follows Islam? The heart of Islamic belief and practice lies in 'the Five Pillars'. These core elements of Islam are as follows.

1. *Faith (Iman)*

The central tenet of Islam is found in the creed: 'There is no god but Allah, and Muhammad is the apostle of God.' A strict monotheistic affirmation that 'God is one' disallows any concept of trinity or any other theology which puts something or someone alongside God. Nevertheless Muslims believe that God said to Muhammad, 'I shall not be mentioned unless you are mentioned with me'. But it should be emphasized that Muslims do not believe that Muhammad was somehow divine. He was a man and definitely not to be equated with God. But he was the supreme and final prophet, the messenger of God. Through him God reveals his will in the Qur'an, the final book of God. Just as Muhammad is said to be the final prophet, superceding all previous messengers of God (Adam, Noah, Abraham, Jesus etc.), so likewise the Qur'an supercedes the three previous divine books – the Law of the prophet Musa (Moses), the Psalms of Da'ud (David) and the Gospel of the prophet Isa (Jesus).

2. *Prayer (Salat)*

Five times a day the pious Muslim must recite the set prayers, and on Friday at midday it is expected that he will do so in the mosque. At prayer times the call to prayer (the *Azan*) will sound out from the minaret of the mosque. Then the Muslim will attend to ritual washings to ensure his purity before coming to prayer. The climax of the prayers is the act of prostration with forehead to the ground as a sign of total submission to

Allah. Words from the Qur'an are recited during the prayers, but the key words are *Allahu Akbar*, God is great.

While these times of prayer form a fixed ritual, and the words are set, the Muslim also prays at other times in his own language and with personal requests.

3. *Alms (Zakat)*

Muslims are expected to give two-and-a-half per cent of their income and of some capital possessions, in charity to the poor.

4. *Fasting (Sawm)*

All healthy Muslims are required to refrain from food and drink, as well as from smoking and sexual relations, in the month of Ramadan from sunrise to sunset. It is thought that the first revelations of the Qur'an were given to Muhammad on the twenty-seventh night of Ramadan, so this is commemorated specially as 'the Night of Blessing'. Pious Muslims therefore make a point of doing good works on each of the odd-numbered nights during the last ten days of Ramadan. They hope that the angel of revelation may see this and reward them. In a tropical climate, maintaining a strict daily fast is a very demanding discipline, but at night Muslims will relax and feast.

5. *Pilgrimage (Haj)*

Once during his lifetime the Muslim should go to Mecca on pilgrimage. Many find this an inspiring experience as they join with multitudes of other Muslims from many countries, sharing together in prayer around the black meteorite stone at the heart of the place of pilgrimage.

Other beliefs

Closely associated with the five pillars of Islam is the concept of Jihad or holy war. Muslims are to be willing to fight in defence of God and Islam. History reveals, however, that holy war has not always been waged in defence, because the honour of Allah and of Islam demands that all people should submit to the truth of God's revelation.

When listing their basic beliefs Muslims will also emphasize *angels* and *judgment*.

Angels are important to Islam, firstly, because it was through an angel that God revealed his books to the prophets. But also, because Islam has only a strict non-trinitarian monotheism, it finds it hard to balance the idea of God's absolute glory and greatness with a belief in God relating to us at our level. The angels act as intermediaries between the supreme God and mere mortals.

The Qur'an repeatedly affirms that God will show mercy to the faithful. Islam therefore has a firm belief in Paradise, the climax of all earthly bliss. Muslims also strongly believe in Hell with all its horrors. Judgment comes after death when our faith and works will be weighed in the divine scales. If our good works outweigh our sins, then God's mercy will probably carry us to Paradise. To claim assurance of salvation is considered a sin, for the sovereign God can assign us to Paradise or Hell as he wishes.

Islamic law (Shari'a)

As Muhammad was not only a prophet but also the state leader in Medina and later in Mecca, Islam relates to every aspect of life. There is no distinction between the secular and the spiritual. An all-embracing system of law therefore developed and was systematized during the eighth and ninth centuries. The law is based on four foundations: the revealed teachings of the Qur'an; the example of the Sunna; analogy of one law with another; and the common agreement or traditional practice of the Muslim community. Legal scholars (*ulama*) determine the interpretation of the law but legal experts (*mufti*) actually pronounce on what is to be practised. Then the Judge (*qadi*) administers the law.

There is considerable debate in the Muslim world on law, particularly with reference to the laws on marriage and divorce, inheritance and criminal penalties. Traditional law has discriminated badly against women, but some countries are adapting the law to improve their status. The traditional practice of public beatings, cutting off of hands and beheading now seem barbaric to many Muslims. Some states still practise full Islamic law, but others have compromised. The current renewal of strict Islam in the Middle East and elsewhere includes a demand for the full practice of *Shari' a*.

Divisions of Islam

God is one; the people of Islam must therefore also be one. This is an important concept to Muslims. So it is a tragic shame for them that Muslim countries are divided and even wage war against each other. Muslims will often claim that there is only one Islam while Christianity is fearfully divided into a multitude of denominations. But Islam too has several divisions. It has two basic groups, the Sunni and the Shi'i. The division occurred just over thirty years after Muhammad's death in AD 632 and was caused by disagreement over the nature of leadership in the Muslim community.

Sunni Islam

The Sunnis' answer to the question of a successor to Muhammad was to select, by consensus of the community, a caliph (meaning 'representative' or 'deputy') from the tribe to which Muhammad belonged. They believed that God would guide the community through their adherence to the law already given in the Qur'an and Sunna. The caliph need only guard that prophetic legacy and administer the community's affairs.

Shiah Islam

Some Muslims believed that Muhammad had intended a much more radical leadership. They looked for a leader, or *Imam*, who could give inspired and infallible interpretations of the Qur'an. Imams would therefore need to be appointed and could not just be 'voted in' by a majority decision. Shiites believe that the authority of the prophet Muhammad was passed down through the fourth caliph, Ali, Muhammad's son-in-law, and then to a succession of Imams. While the Shiites particularly look back with reverence to Ali, they also highly esteem his son who was killed as a martyr by other Muslims in battle. Shiites therefore have a strong sense of the honour of being allowed to die as a martyr for their faith. This encourages an apparently reckless spirit of self-sacrifice on behalf of the faith, evidenced in particular in Shiite 'suicide missions' in Lebanon, against Israel, and in Iran's war against Iraq.

The Ismaili sect of Shiite Muslims believe that the seventh Imam never died, but still lives in spiritual form and will come back as the *Mahdi* (a sort of messianic figure) to restore true Islam and righteousness. Other Shiite Muslims believe it was the twelfth Imam who still lives and will come again.

The vast majority of Muslims (about ninety per cent) are orthodox Sunnis, but the Shiites form the next largest group. Shiah Islam is the national religion of Iran under Khomeini and also has followers in most of the Gulf states, in India, Pakistan, Syria and Iraq.

Wahhabi

This ultra-orthodox movement started in the eighteenth century. Though its adherents consider themselves to be orthodox Sunnis, they have their own distinct identity. The Wahhabis captured Mecca in 1806 and they now rule in Saudi Arabia. They protest against all modern innovations in the practice of Islam and call for a return to the purity of a faith based on the Qur'an alone. They do not allow the mention of Muhammad or any other human being or angel in prayer, reckoning this to be idolatry. Music and tobacco are rejected; mosques and personal dress must be very simple with no gold ornaments. All forms of superstition in religion (prayer at saints' tombs, for example) are utterly rejected.

Ahmadiyya

Started by Mirza Gulam Ahmad in the Punjab in the late nineteenth century, this strongly missionary movement has spread
rapidly. It has pioneered the development of Islam in Britain
and other European countries, but is outlawed by other
Muslims and considered a non-Muslim sect. Ahmadiyyas
differ from other Muslims in the following ways:

- They deny that apostasy from Islam should be punished by
  death.
- Jihad or holy war is, they say, to be waged only by peaceful
  means, not by violence. They stress obedience to govern-
  ments.
- They believe that Gulam Ahmad was a reincarnation of
  Jesus, Muhammad and Krishna. He will return as the final
  Mahdi, but will bring in righteousness by peaceful means
  only.
- They deny that Jesus died on the cross, claiming that he only
  fainted and recovered after his burial. He then walked to
  Kashmir where he lived to the age of 120 and was buried.

Sufis

These are the mystics of Islam, stressing devotion to God and
an intimate relationship with him. They struggle against being
bound to this world and therefore emphasize poverty, fasting,
celibacy, all-night prayer and a serious sense of sin. Some talk
of 'exquisite suffering' through the meeting of God's mercy
with man's spiritual poverty.

There has been a tendency among them to emphasize God
as the only ultimate reality and God's total indwelling of people. This has led to some saying that God is the same as man.
Thus the tenth-century Hallaj claimed, 'I am he whom I love,
and he whom I love is I'.

Some Sufis (the Dervishes for instance) have used various
dubious means to induce a state of trance and thus a sense that
they have achieved a mystical oneness with God. Trance-inducing

dance and constantly repeated song and music are particularly common.

For some years it seemed that Sufism would be utterly rejected by orthodox Muslims, but through the theological and mystical work of the great Al-Ghazzali (1059-1111) Sufism has lived side by side with other branches of Islam and influenced its whole life. It is particularly common in the Indian sub-continent.

Folk Islam

This is not a separate division of Islam, but the popular, superstitious practices and beliefs which permeate all forms of Islam. The spirit world is very close to the surface in the life of many Muslims.

Magic charms, curses, the evil eye, the hand of Fatima (daughter of Muhammad), texts from the Qur'an itself – all are commonly used to bring healing, to avenge an enemy or to ward off evil. In some countries the traditional witch-doctor figure has been incorporated into the Islamic system. In others, spirit mediums practise their skills. This often leads to occult spiritism which presents dangers to Christians who witness in Muslim societies. In relating to Islam and to Muslims the Christian must always bear in mind the realities of spiritual warfare and draw on the grace and power of Jesus who has defeated all demonic powers by his cross and resurrection.

Christian witness

It is helpful to remember the following points in talking with Muslims about Jesus.

a. *The Crusades*. Muslims remember the bitter history of the Crusades and of Imperialistic expansion when Christians fought with power against Muslims. They think of Christians as militant and unloving, people of power but not humility. Loyal friendship from a Christian will be vital if a Muslim is to be able to overcome his natural prejudice against Christianity.

b. *Final revelation*. They think of the Qur'an as God's final revelation and Muhammad as the ultimate prophet, so it does not generally occur to them that they could go back to the former religion of Christianity – just as Christians would never think of going back to Judaism. We need to show how the Old Testament Scriptures pointed forward to Christ alone as the supreme Lord, and also need to help the Muslim see what unique claims Jesus made for himself.

c. *The community*. The community of the people of Islam is very strong. Pressure against leaving the community is immense. We have seen that Islam is more than just a religion, it is a whole social system. It is also strongly political. If you change your religion, you move out of that whole social and political community. You lose your family, job, friends and nationality. As witnesses to Muslims we need to be totally willing to share with them our own homes, families and friends should their own reject them for becoming Christians. We need to be prepared to offer very practical care and hospitality.

d. *Bible and Qu'ran*. The Bible is very different from the Qur'an. To Muslims it seems too human to be inspired by God, as it is obviously written by humans. It may be wise to start by encouraging a Muslim friend to read Luke's Gospel and Acts because they have parallels with Muslim ideas of Jesus, particularly in the stories of Jesus' birth and childhood.

e. *Jesus*. Muslims believe in Jesus as a prophet, but know relatively little about him. They believe in his virgin birth and ascension, but not in his death on the cross or his divinity. It may be wise to help Muslims to get to know the human Jesus and love him before confronting the issue of his divinity. At first, then, we should introduce Muslims to the stories of Jesus' life on earth, and to his teaching.

e. *Forgiveness*. Muslims see no need of Jesus' sacrificial death for our sins because they feel the all-powerful God can forgive sins without such sacrifice if he so wishes. We need to be sensitive to their feeling, but also point out the Bible's teaching that while God's judgment of sin is certain for all people, his forgiveness is freely given to all who trust in Jesus' death as punishment on their behalf. We will need to talk through how impossible it is to earn God's favour by anything we do.

f. *'Son of God'*. Muslims like to quote a simple mathematical formula against the doctrine of the Trinity: $1+1+1 = 3$. It does not equal one! Christians need to do their homework on the deity of Christ and on the Trinity! Muslims will also attack the idea that Jesus was God's son, saying that it is blasphemy to claim that God took a wife and had a son. We need, then to be careful to explain what we mean by the title 'Son of God'.

Witness to Muslims will often take great patience and gentle love – both of which must persist despite rejection. But quiet friendship will allow us to share our knowledge of God through Jesus Christ and, gradually, the Holy Spirit can use our witness to bring people to a saving faith in Jesus. The Christian message of undeserved grace and forgiving love can break down all barriers. We can trust God that constant, faithful prayer will not be in vain.

Discussion starters

1. What do Muslims believe about the Qur'an as God's word? Where do their views of the Qur'an differ from the Christian's view of the Bible?

2. Why do Christians believe that there could never be a prophet greater than Jesus? (See Hebrews 1:1-4.) Why would a Muslim reject this belief?

3. Why is it important to Muslims that 'God is One'? How would you explain that God is One, but in three persons?

4. Compare the 'five pillars' of Islam with Christian teaching and practice. Is there anything you think Christians can learn from these?

5. How could you use each of the 'five pillars' to explain something of your faith to a Muslim?

6. If you have Muslim friends, ask them what Allah is like. How does their description compare with the biblical revelation of the nature of God? Where does it differ?

7. What Christian teaching about Jesus Christ do Muslims not accept? What do you think they miss out on as a result?

Hinduism

Hinduism is the umbrella word which covers the great variety of religious beliefs among the Indian peoples. In talking of this variety in Hinduism, K.C. Sen in his book, *Hinduism*, says: 'The number of paths to the One Infinite is necessarily infinite . . . there is in it monism, dualism, monotheism, polytheism, pantheism.' The former Indian president and influential Hindu philosopher, Radhakrishnan, wrote that, 'the theist and the atheist, sceptic and agnostic may all be Hindus'. And yet there is a unity which links the many streams of Hinduism together.

One factor which unites them is the belief that there is no absolute or exclusive truth. The Hindu will therefore be very tolerant of people who have different approaches to religion, as long as the other person does not claim any *unique, exclusive* truth. The Hindu is tolerant of tolerance, but can be quite intolerant of any belief in an absolute truth. Another common belief is that facts belong only to the surface of things; it is ideas that count. Reality lies beyond what we see around us, beyond historical facts.

Western thinking has been much influenced by these beliefs. Many today reject any absolute claims to truth which imply that another religion's revelation may not be true. Tolerance is more important than truth. Some Christian theologians, as well as other writers, are talking about the importance of ideas rather than facts. For instance, some say that it does not matter whether Jesus actually rose from the dead; what is significant is the spiritual idea of resurrection and new life from death.

We will look at five main aspects of Hindu philosophy and culture.

One ultimate reality

The highest form of Hindu philosophy, Advaita Hinduism, is found in the writings of Sankara (about AD 788-850) who expounded the scriptures known as the Upanishads. He maintained that Brahman is the only ultimate reality. There is no concept of a good God versus an evil opponent. Nor, in this school of thought, is there the concept of the soul maintaining its individuality after it has been released from the world of nature. While Brahman is the ultimate cause of all things he/it is not personal – but also not impersonal. Brahman is the indescribable and formless 'ground of being'. Brahman is sometimes described as 'neti, neti' – not this, not this. Whatever one says about Brahman is not true. Brahman has no attributes or characteristics and yet is, in the last resort, the only final reality. Everything except Brahman is illusion (*maya*). A traditional story illustrates what this means. It is a story about a man who saw a coil of rope in the twilight and thought it was a snake, so showing that there are three levels of existence:

1. *The snake*
In the mind of that man the snake was real. He reacted as if the snake were there and so did and said things in response to the apparent fact of the snake. Those words and deeds influenced the course of his family's life.

2. *The rope*
By the light of day the unreality of the snake became clear and it was seen to be actually a coil of rope. Most of us live with the belief that the rope is true reality. We can see it, feel it, analyse it. It seems obvious that the rope is reality. But Sankara's school of Hindu philosophy says that actually nothing exists except Brahman. Not only the snake, but also the rope is an illusion. And indeed the man who sees the snake or rope is

also just illusory. Nothing is, except Brahman. There is nothing other than Brahman. All is Brahman.

2. *Brahman*

In claiming that all is Brahman, the Upanishads further state that Brahman is found within all people and all things. In all living things there is a spirit, soul or self which is called the Atman, but neither we nor anything else has an existence of its own: the self, or Atman, is really Brahman. The search for Brahman is therefore within ourselves, though we do not exist as separate entities. So ultimate truth is that neither the rope, the snake nor the man and his family exist. Brahman alone is ultimate truth.

There is therefore no duality or separate existence. We cannot talk of 'you and me', 'this and that'. Such words bring division and tension based on ignorance (*avidya*), for they fail to appreciate that nothing is except Brahman. All ego-feeling is *avidya*. This contrasts sharply with the Jewish and Christian view of creation, which emphasizes the separateness of God from the world which he has created.

While it may be a great aim in life to realize that there is no separate self-existence and that nothing has reality except Brahman, it is in fact difficult to live in this way. In normal daily life such a belief becomes impracticable. Even the practice of religion – worship, prayer and devotion – is negated by the teachings of the religion in two ways. First, all these religious practices demand a duality – the real existence of two things: the worshipper and that which is worshipped. Second, an indescribable, non-personal Absolute does not inspire loving devotion. These problems have led to the development of forms of Hinduism which are able to attract the devotion of the multitudes of India.

Religious devotion

In the Advaita Hinduism considered above, the absolute Brahman is considered to be indescribable and without any attributes or characteristics. This is known as Brahman Nirguna. But, as we have seen, it is impossible to relate in worship or adoration to such a being. A further development therefore emerged through a great twelfth-century philosopher, Ramanuja, and through the great epic scriptures, the Mahabharata and the Ramayana. Within the Mahabharata is found the much loved and often quoted Bhagavadgita which is the most influential Hindu scripture in modern India. Although the concept of the indefinable Brahman remained as the highest form of Hinduism and as the goal of Hindu devotion, it was now taught that there was also a form of Brahman which does have attributes and can be personal. This more personalized form of Brahman relates closely to traditional ideas of religion in ancient India. These very early beliefs are embodied in the scriptures called the Vedas which date from as early as 2000 BC. In these early times people believed in a variety of nature gods, such as Rudra, the storm god, Surya the sun god or Agni the fire god.

Bhakti Hinduism, the religion of devotion, began to flourish between AD 300 and 1200. During this time four gods in particular came to be the objects of Bhakti: Siva, Sakti, Vishnu and Lakshmi.

Siva is the god of death and destruction, but also of compassion. He not only sends sickness, but also heals. He is often portrayed with a snake round his neck and dancing the dance of death. This is because he is said to have swallowed poison during a battle. But he is also deemed to have power to recreate out of death. The linga, a symbol of the male sex organ, is associated with him identifying him with rebirth and fertility.

Sakti is the female god of creative power. It is through the power of Sakti that the creative word comes into being. She is the mother goddess. Her worship is sometimes linked to animal sacrifice.

In this type of Hinduism the one ultimate Absolute (the Trimurti) consists of three beings: Brahman the creator, Vishnu the sustainer, and Siva the destroyer. The personalized Brahman is particularly reverenced in the second form of the ultimate Absolute, the god Vishnu and his wife Lakshmi.

Vishnu comes down to earth in various incarnations (*avatara*), of which ten are celebrated. The best known incarnation is Krishna, the black and beautiful one; but there are nine others, including a swan, dwarf and fish.

Bhakti is also paid to a great number of other forms of Brahman. This is what leads to the common statement that in Hinduism literally millions of different divinities are worshipped, and idol figures abound. In India temples with idols of these various aspects of Brahman are to be found in every village and community. The European will often be shocked by this multiplicity of idols and the devotion paid to them. Many of the idol forms seem grotesque and, by European standards, are often ugly and sensual. Some of the most common ones are related to Ganesh, partly elephant and partly human, and to Hanuman the monkey god.

These gods are given elaborate worship not only in the temples but also in the homes. The family shrine with its particular god will be the centre of family devotion. The gods are also the centre of excited public worship when they are paraded around the local area in their annual festival. Siva has his public festival in early spring (the *Holi* Festival) which is often called the Water Festival because scented water is splashed on passers-by in liberal quantities. As might be expected with the worship of Siva, the phallic symbol is given great prominence portraying the fertility of spring. Vishnu and Lakshmi are honoured in the New Year holiday of *Diwali*, while the early autumn *Dasera* festival celebrates the victory of Rama as recounted in the great Ramayana epic scriptures.

As a sign of devotion to the gods Hindus will often submit themselves to severe ascetic practices – such as climbing very long sets of stone steps on their knees, or taking a vow to keep silence for a number of years. Through their devotion they hope to gain sufficient merit to move on to a higher stage of reincarnation when they might attain enlightenment. Through his devotion a devotee may receive extra status. Devout Hindus fast regularly to receive extra blessings, or protection against evil, from their gods.

Release from existence

The Hindu's ideal is to gain release from separate self-existence and become one with Brahman. This means that he has to break out of the continuous chain of reincarnation. The Hindu claims that one life leads to another which, in its turn, leads on to yet another. *Samsara* or reincarnation, goes on eternally. Whether his next reincarnation is better or worse than his present one, will depend on his *karma* or actions. Karma is often defined as the law of cause and effect. Everything has its results – and these results will in their turn cause further repercussions. So every good or bad word or deed goes on in its effects for ever, like ripples spreading from a stone that falls into the water. If the Hindu's deeds are good, he may ascend higher towards the goal of enlightenment. If his deeds are bad, then he will fall still lower in his next incarnation. If he accumulates enough good karma, then he may eventually become a *sannyasi*, someone who is spiritually ready to be enlightened and sink into the great Brahman.

Like a drop of water sinking into a great ocean, so a person loses his own identity to merge into Brahman. This end state is called *Nirvana*, the state in which he has no further personal being and where there is no duality of 'I and you', 'this and that'. No further tensions exist because only Brahman remains.

Three routes to release from existence, and into Nirvana, are taught. All three are considered valid, though some schools of thought will believe one way to be better than the others.

The way of knowledge (Jnana Marga)

This way of enlightenment is particularly stressed by Advaita (non-dualist) Hinduism. When one knows or understands that Brahman alone is ultimate reality, then release from existence may be experienced. Meanwhile the problem is ignorance (*avidva*) or failure to understand.

The way of right conduct (Karma Marga)

The way of knowledge has been described by one Hindu as 'dry and hard', and is generally taken up only by an intellectual minority. But the way of right conduct is more down-to-earth and practical. It is not easy, however, to define just what is included in the karma. Clearly it includes basic moral behaviour both as an individual and within society. Vegetarianism is an important part of it. Most Hindus would say it includes following the rules of caste which we shall look at later in this chapter; it is also important to fulfil one's responsibilities to others, especially family members. The law of non-violence (*ahimsa*) was considered central to karma by such leaders as Gandhi and Nehru. Karma relates also to ritual practices associated with the worship of the gods in the temples and in the home. By all these means one develops good karma or merit.

The way of devotion (Bhakti Marga)

As we have already seen, there is a further reaction against just the 'dry and hard' non-dualist way, namely the way of devotion. Hindus express warmth of worship, prayer and adoration in their relationship to the incarnations of Vishnu and the gods who are represented by the many idols. Because the Hindu is more interested in ideas than facts, it is not important whether these gods have any historical reality or actually exist. Thus Gandhi wrote: 'Rama, Krishna etc. are called incarnations of God because we attribute to them divine qualities. In truth they are creations of man's imagination. Whether they actually lived on earth does not affect the picture of them in men's minds.' Though Gandhi would not be regarded by Hindus as a specially enlightened person or 'guru', his observation is a legitimate description of their thought. This lack of concern for historical accuracy stands in direct contrast to the concerns of the New Testament where the historicity of Jesus Christ is underlined. However, the sense of personal unworthiness, and of trust in God and surrender to him, are common to both Bhakti Hinduism and Christianity. This common ground has in the past formed a 'bridge' by which Hindus have come to faith in Christ.

The Caste system

There is uncertainty about how caste divisions first became a part of Indian society, but the system probably originated with the invasion of the sub-continent from the north in the very early history of India. The invaders came from central Asia and were lighter skinned than the original inhabitants of India, whom they drove south. Still today north Indians are often lighter in skin colour than the people of south India, although this is by no means always the case. Many scholars suggest that the word for caste originates from the word for colour, indicating that the conquering light-skinned Aryans became the upper caste while the original dark-skinned Dravidians were forced to submit to them as a lower-caste people. Certainly the idea of caste came into Hinduism very early, for it is first mentioned in the Rig Veda scriptures.

Four basic castes were established during this time. The *Brahmin* were the priests and religious teachers. The *Kshatriya* were the kings, warriors and aristocrats. The *Vaisya* were the middle-class merchants and traders. The *Sudra* were the peasant farmers and servants.

Outside the caste system altogether live the *Harijans*, the untouchables, who are from a Hindu point of view unclean and have virtually no rights. They are seen as unclean because in their work they have to come into contact with 'unclean' things – a leather worker comes into contact with dead animals; a sweeper comes into contact with human and animal waste. This is in real contrast to biblical teaching, which affirms that all people are to be valued because all are made in the image of God. The Bible goes further, denouncing all barriers of status between people – black and white, man and woman, white collar and artisan.

The caste system does not allow inter-marriage or any social relationships with those of other castes. You may not eat or drink with someone of a lower caste. Although the Indian government has tried to break down these strict barriers and bring a greater justice and equality into society, in practice people generally hold on to them firmly.

The Reform movement in Hinduism

The nineteenth century saw the start of a new Reform movement in Hinduism which strongly influences Indian life today. Ram Mohan Roy (1772-1833) was widely read with a thorough knowledge of the Hindu, Muslim and Christian Scriptures. He was influenced by the ethical teaching of Jesus in the Gospels and his social reforms earned him the reputation of being the father of modern India. He was followed by Keshab Chandra Sen (1838-1884) who continued Roy's search for a universal religion. He was particularly attracted to the person of Jesus. But the doctrines of the Trinity and of Jesus' divinity were a barrier to either of them becoming Christian. They also found the very foreign character of the church to be repugnant.

Gradually, however, some external forms of Christian worship crept into these new movements of Hinduism. I remember hearing a large crowd of Indian children singing choruses in what appeared to be a Christian childrens' meeting, but then discovered that it was a Hindu gathering!

The Reform movement was continued by Vivekananda (1863-1902) and by great poets like Rabindranath Tagore (1861-1949). Under the influence of Europeans and of Christianity they sought to bring Hinduism into a more modern approach to life and thought, opposing suttee (the burning of widows on their husband's funeral pyre), and animal sacrifice. The extremes of Hindu ritual also came under attack from them. Yet this reform was built on the foundation of traditional Hinduism and even developed the slogan 'Back to the Vedas'. Sen has influenced some streams of Christian theology by his emphasis on the traditional Hindu idea that the one

Brahman is also the three-fold Saccidananda. Saccidananda is composed of Sat (Being), Cit (Truth) and Ananda (Joy). Some Christian thinkers, particularly the great nineteenth-century theologian Brahmabandhab Upadhyaya, came to describe the Christian God in parallel terms.

Christian witness

The following are some points to be aware of when talking with Hindus about Jesus and the Christian faith.

The unique status of Jesus

A young Indian lady came for counselling after the appeal at a Christian church. Yes, she definitely wanted to receive Jesus as saviour and Lord. Yes, she understood what it meant for Jesus to die on the cross for her sin and rise to give her new life. The Christians rejoiced. Then I was asked to come across and talk further with her. I soon discovered that she had not grasped that faith in Jesus denies faith in other gods and saviours. She demonstrated a common misunderstanding of Jesus' claim to be the only true God. She would have been happy to add him to the pantheon of Hindu deities. It is hard for a Hindu to realize that the claims of Christ are exclusive and unique. While never compromising on the uniqueness of Jesus Christ, we need also to show that we are not proudly intolerant. Our emphasis must be on the absolute and incomparable perfection of Jesus Christ and of his work for us.

The concept of eternal life

The Bible promises that believers in Jesus will have eternal life. To the Hindu that is a threat, not a promise! His aim is to gain release from the constant existence that comes from reincarnation. He already has eternal life as a Hindu and longs to escape from it. As Christians we need to explain what we mean by eternal life and why it is desirable. We can, for instance, describe eternal life as being the release from Samsara, the cycle of rebirth, so that we can live in the presence of God.

Jesus' lack of 'enlightenment'

Jesus often said of himself, 'I am' – the good shepherd, the door, the way, the truth and life. We have seen that in Hinduism to claim such real existence demonstrates that person's ignorance. All existence is an illusion. If Jesus were truly enlightened, he would say 'I am not'. We have to explain that God exists as a being separate from his creation, that he made mankind to be like him in having individual identity and existence. The created world, too, is genuinely real, and the Christian's hope for the future is to live in the presence of God in a completely transformed, real world.

The idea of being born again

John's Gospel declares, 'you must be born again'. At puberty, the upper-caste Brahmin boy is given a special string as a mark of his caste status. Westernized Hindus use the term, 'born again' for this event. Our use of the term will easily be misunderstood unless we take care to explain what we mean. It is usually better to speak of conversion in terms of making a public declaration of the lordship of Christ, or of his being our only saviour.

The practical and spiritual

Hindus tend to find themselves caught between two worlds and two sets of values. Because they do not consider this world to be ultimately real, an unwashed holy man may be more respected than an efficient, Western-style evangelist with his briefcase. Yet many modern Indians also long for material prosperity, social justice and progress. We need to demonstrate, by our teaching and by our practical involvement in society's concerns, that the Christian faith is both spiritual and practical. Our lifestyle must show that a living communion with God through prayer is matched by a shared concern with the creator for the well-being of his creation.

The origin of life

The theory of reincarnation teaches that there is no final end to life and that there was never any ultimate beginning. The Buddha said that 'all is a wheel of becoming'. And yet the question remains, 'how did it all begin?' The Christian can agree with the Hindu about the necessity of something in the universe that is never-ending, and can point to the biblical account of creation which speaks powerfully of an eternal God who always was and always will be. His creation, by contrast, is finite and limited, created for a purpose, and will one day come to an end.

The idea of a personal God

We noted that Hinduism sees the indescribable, non-attributed Brahman as higher than any personal or attributed idea of Brahman. But the Christian faith affirms definitely that God is personal. We even list his attributes – all-powerful, all-holy, the God of love, and so on. And we underline the fact that Jesus is a historical figure and the events of his life and death are facts. To the Advaita Hindu this shows that Christianity is shallow and does not enter the deeper realms of Brahman. These are a tiny minority in Britain, however; most British Hindus try to reach God through *bhakti* or devotion. They *do* have a concept of a God who is personal, just and holy. They also have an awareness of sin, not only in a ceremonial sense but in the ethics of life. These understandings of God can be built on by the Christian in his or her witness.

Christian lifestyle

Devout Hindus find it hard to come to terms with the fact that a Christian can be a non-vegetarian and 'godly' at the same time. For them, loving God means not killing his creation. We should be careful not to give offence here.

A positive approach

Hindus are attracted towards Christian fellowships where God is at work in a special way through signs and wonders. Perhaps the majority of Hindu converts have turned to Christ not because of any theological convictions but because of the love and openness of Christians and because of the general atmosphere of worship they experienced in Christian meetings. They admire and long for a spiritual experience of God. They are attracted to a place where God is 'at work'.

Discussion starters

1. Make a list of Hindu words used in this chapter and discuss what they mean.

2. Hinduism denies any absolute truths and is more interested in ideas than facts. How important do you think 'truth' is and how would you talk to a Hindu about the truth of Christianity?

3. What aspects of the Hindu religion do you find attractive, and why? How might they form bridges for a Hindu to understand Christianity?

4. What aspects of the Hindu religion do you feel are in direct opposition to Christian teaching? Why? How would you explain Christian teaching on these things?

5. How would you explain to a Hindu that it is not wrong for a devout Christian to be a non-vegetarian?

6. Do you know anyone who believes in reincarnation? Why do they think this way? What can we learn from the Bible about life after death? (See, for example, 1 Corinthians 15:1-8,12-24 and 35-57; Hebrews 9:27-28; 2 Corinthians 5:1-10.)

6

Sikhism

Before the 1950s Sikhism was considered an ethnic religion of Northern India and little was known about it in Britain or the USA. After the Second World War and the founding of the independent countries of India and Pakistan many Sikhs arrived in Britain, Canada and the USA. Local papers recorded the problem of whether Sikh bus conductors and drivers should be allowed to wear turbans instead of uniform caps. Later the same questions arose over enforcing the law about safety helmets. Now in the streets and schools of many British cities Asian men with their hair in turbans and boys with their hair tied on the top of the head with a handkerchief, are a familiar sight. But there will also be many non-observant Sikhs who will have had their hair cut. In the 1980s the Sikhs were again in the news because of a militant movement which wanted an independent state in the Punjab, India. After ten years of fighting the movement was squashed by the Indian authorities. In the late 1990s Sikhs were again in the news in Canada, the US and Britain because of a dispute over furniture in their temples. Since they emphasise the equality of all people their tradition was for all to sit on the floor. As they settled in colder countries many Sikh temples acquired tables and chairs. Some conservatives began to complain and excommunicate those whom they saw as more liberal!

We will now look at the origin of this religious group.

Political and spiritual history

Just south of the Himalayas and north of Delhi in north-western India there is a geographical area known as the Punjab, an extensive plain watered by five rivers. In the fifteenth century the inhabitants of the Punjab were either Hindu or Muslim. There was great hatred and jealousy between the two groups and the Hindus were persecuted by their Muslim rulers. Some became dissatisfied with both religions and became *Sikhs* — meaning disciples – of a teacher, Guru Nanak.

Nanak (1469-1539) was born into a Hindu family but he rejected the caste system, idolatry, the worship of many gods and the rituals. He taught that God is one and that only he should be worshipped, that all humans are equal, and that all men and women can know God and should devote themselves to him and to good actions. The origins of his teaching can be found in Bhakti Hinduism, the religion of devotion, and in the monotheistic mysticism of the Sufi form of Islam. He was opposed by the high-caste priestly Brahmins and the Muslim leaders because their authority was threatened by his teaching. Yet he himself never planned to found another religion; he sought to unite those who loved God and wanted to serve their fellow men. To this day Sikhs do not seek to proselytize and they respect those of other faiths who worship God and seek to do good. All the Hindu scriptures were in Sanskrit and the Qur'an of the Muslims was in Arabic but Nanak taught in the local language of the Punjabi.

When he died in 1539 his teaching was continued by Guru Angad (1504-1522). Angad is said to have collected together all Nanak's hymns, but to have added only a small number (about thirteen) himself. He stressed the need for education for all, using the local language. This meant that religion and learning would be available to everyone, not just priests. Today among the Sikhs there is still a high emphasis on education and recently there has been a new desire for Sikh children born in Britain to learn Punjabi so that they will not be denied knowledge of their religious and cultural heritage.

The third Sikh Guru, Amar Das (1479-1574), reinforced the teaching of the equality of all by attaching a free kitchen – *langar* – to all Sikh places of worship. People of all religions and every caste could eat there. When the Moghul Emperor, Akbar, visited the Guru he was expected to eat in the kitchen first with all the ordinary people, including so-called 'untouchables'. There is still a langar in every Gurdwara, or Sikh temple. Sikhs give money to support these kitchens and today the poor and the unemployed can eat there.

The fourth Guru of Sikhism, Ram Das (1534-1581), founded the modern city of Amritsar around 'the pool of immortality'. It attracted many people and soon became a large centre of trade. Today it is a city of half a million people. The fifth Guru, Arjan (1563-1606), began building the Golden Temple there in 1589. It was built with a door on each of the four sides to show that all people are welcome of whatever caste or faith. It is still the centre of Sikh religious and national life. It is also the home of many of the militant Sikhs who want the state of Punjab to become independent of India.

Guru Arjan also wrote many hymns. He collected these and the hymns of the previous Gurus, compiling from them an authoritative holy book known as the *Adi Granth*, or 'first collection'. This was installed in the Golden Temple at Amritsar. The tenth Guru, Gobind Singh (1666-1708), added to this the writings of later Gurus. Shortly before his death he conferred on these scriptures the title of guru, and these were then known as the *Guru Granth Sahib*. This changed the structure of Sikhism, as the sequence of gurus ended and the scriptures took over their role as the sole authority. So today the Guru Granth Sahib has pride of place in every Gurdwara and in many Sikh homes.

The Sikhs, unlike the Hindus, did not consider it a sin to cross the Indus river. As they became wealthy through their trading links, notably through trade in Turkish horses, they came into conflict with the Muslim rulers of India. Guru Arjan was imprisoned as the leader of 'this heresy and false cult' and, in 1606,was tortured to death. His martyrdom led to an influx of believers from the Hindu farming community, who were also suffering at the hands of the Muslim rulers.

Until the violent death of the Guru Arjan the Sikhs had been a peace-loving community but now they accepted that they had a right to defend their faith and community with military force. The sixth Guru, Hargobind, established a stable of 800 horses and enlisted 300 horsemen and 60 artillery in his service. They defended themselves successfully in battle but they did not claim any territory.

After the death of the sixth Guru, the seventh and eighth lived peacefully and the ninth, Tegh Bahadur, was also a devotional man rather than a soldier. But when the Muslim emperor of Delhi demanded that the Brahmins in Kashmir convert to Islam they asked the Guru to support them. Tegh Bahadur tried to dissuade the emperor from his policy but was charged with sedition and heresy, and was beheaded in 1675. He was succeeded by his nine-year-old son, Gobind Singh. It was at this time that many of the Hindus in the Punjab joined the Sikhs in response to the Muslim persecution.

Guru Gobind Singh, the tenth Guru, founded the *Khalsa*. This was a brotherhood and army, free of caste, colour and social prejudice, formed to fight against tyranny and injustice. He prescribed five symbols for Khalsa Sikhs, known as the Five Ks:

Kesh: uncut hair and beard, as a sign of devotion to God and group identity.

Kangha: a comb, a sign of cleanliness and discipline.

Kara: a metal bangle, originally a mark of restraint and indebtedness to the Guru, also symbolizing the unity of God and the unity with the brotherhood.

Kaccha: shorts, enabling freedom of movement in battle and symbolizing chastity.

Kirpan: a dagger or sword, symbolizing authority, justice and resistance to evil.

When disciples were initiated into the Khalsa the men took the name *Singh* meaning lion, and the women were given the name *Kaur*, meaning princess. Today you will find that these are common names in Sikh families.

Many Sikhs lost their lives in fighting for their faith and in 1708 Guru Gobind Singh himself was stabbed to death by government spies. There was then severe fighting in the Punjab between the Sikhs and the Muslims until 1765, when the Sikh Empire was established. The Sikhs allowed Muslims and Hindus to serve in their government. In 1845 trouble arose between the British Army and the Sikhs; the Sikhs were defeated and their territory was annexed by the British.

In the 1940s they joined with the Indian National Congress to fight against the British. When India gained independence in 1947 their territory, the Punjab, was divided between Muslim Pakistan and Hindu India. As a result, millions of Sikhs were driven out of the fertile area of West Punjab in Pakistan. Now without a state of their own, many have emigrated and settled in countries all over the world.

Beliefs

God is one

The basis of Sikh belief is that God is one. He is the creator of the world, transcendent and immanent, the eternal truth. Guru Nanak's sacred chant about God not only comes at the beginning of their scriptures, but also at the beginning of each of its thirty-one sections. It is known as the Mool Mantra:

'There is one God, Eternal Truth is His Name;
Maker of all things, immanent in all things;
Fearing nothing and at enmity with nothing,
Timeless is His image:
Not begotten, being of His own being,
By the grace of the Guru, made known to Men.'

The Gurus did not claim to be incarnations of God but humans who became very spiritual, as others can become if they follow the Gurus' teaching. Man is made in the image of God. He should seek to commune with God and to withstand self-centredness which separates him from God. Selfishness, anger, covetousness, lust and pride are the most serious sins and not only do they separate man from God but they also destroy his relationship with his fellow man. The Sikh is expected to replace these with self-control, forgiveness, contentment, love of God and humility. Then he should work hard, share his earnings, help the weak and serve the community in every way possible.

The first volume of the Sikh scriptures, the Guru Granth Sahib, is a collection of hymns of the ten Gurus and other writers, including Hindus and Muslims, so it is difficult to construct a Sikh theology. In some hymns there are traces of Hindu mythology and pantheism and the respect shown for the Gurus verges on their being described as divine: 'God himself assumed the form of Nanak . . . the invisible became visible'. In Sikh homes there are pictures of Guru Nanak and the other Gurus, and sometimes incense is burned in front of them. But at its roots Sikhism is monotheistic, even if its practice may have strayed from this ideal.

Evolution of the soul

Sikhs believe in the evolution of the soul. The soul is not predestined; what a person does in this life, good or bad, will affect his soul. If a person persists in evil actions, he will find himself in an endless cycle of birth and death until he repents and deserves God's grace. But if a person does good deeds and calls upon the name of God, God is merciful and can deliver him from the effect of his bad deeds. There is not a great interest in the afterlife, for a Sikh, like the Gurus before him, can attain salvation in this life by devoting himself to God and the service of his fellow men.

The human race as one

As the Sikhs teach that God is one, they also teach that the human race is one. Neither colour, caste, creed, sex nor any other artificial barriers should divide mankind. In a Sikh community there is complete equality between the sexes in political and religious matters; women can visit the temple, conduct services, read the scriptures and pray, just the same as men. They can vote in elections and are even allowed to lead an army. Traditionally parents arrange marriages but the young people including the girls are usually allowed to be involved in the decision. Sikhs are opposed to the caste system of Hinduism but, sadly, where there are large communities of Sikhs in this country there will be different Gurdwaras for different groups. The differences often date back to their former occupations in the Punjab. Marriages are arranged within the group rather than across the groups.

Religious practices

Sikhs do not have to observe special days or festivals. In India they will often meet on the first day of the month. But in countries where Sunday is a rest day they might go to their temples every Sunday. Any day can be a feast or a fast day but on three of the main Hindu festivals the Gurus called the Sikhs together to avoid their being involved in Hindu celebrations. These festivals – Baisakhi, Diwali and Holi – are celebrated by Sikhs, but with distinct differences in emphasis from their Hindu counterparts. They also celebrate the birthdays of Guru Nanak and Guru Gobind Singh and observe the deaths of the fifth and ninth Gurus. On these days they will take out the Granth Sahib in procession around the neighbourhood.

In the same way the Sikhs do not have to keep set times of prayer and are encouraged to call on the name of God and recite the hymns of their faith at any time. Many Sikhs will rise early in the morning, bathe and then read the morning prayer, *Japji*, composed by Guru Nanak. In the evening they will recite *Rahiras*, and at night they will repeat the hymn, *Sohila*.

Baptism or initiation into the Khalsa can take place at any age but not usually before the age of fourteen. In India most Sikhs would be initiated but in Britain fewer would be

baptized in this way. The ceremony is conducted by five elders of the community in the Gurdwara. They take some water
and sugar, *amrit*, in a bowl and say five prayers from the Guru
Granth Sahib. Having stirred the water with a double-edged
sword, *Khanda*, they sprinkle it on the candidates and offer it
to them to drink. The initiates agree to adopt the five Ks and
are instructed not to remove any hair from their body, not to
use tobacco or take drugs or alcohol, not to eat meat killed in
the Muslim manner and not to commit adultery.

The Sikh way of life

At a Sikh marriage ceremony the couple are seated in front of
the Guru Granth Sahib in the temple. The responsibilities of
marriage are explained to them, four hymns from the Granth
are read or sung and the couple walk round the book four
times. Since the whole ceremony takes place in front of their
Holy Book they believe no marriage document is needed.

As we noted earlier, the Guru Granth Sahib is now the
Sikh's guide through life and it is always treated with reverence. It holds the central position in the Gurdwara, in the
home, at festivals, in the marriage service and also at the nam-
ing of a newborn child and at a time of mourning. When Sikhs
die, they are cremated and the relatives and friends mourn for
ten days. During this period much of the Granth will be read.
On special occasions the whole of the Granth is read by a team
of readers without stopping, which takes forty-eight hours.
When a Sikh moves to a new home, sets out on a journey,
opens a shop, starts a business or gathers in the harvest, the
Granth is read. Its reading marks every important occasion.
Because Sikhs bow to the Granth in their temples and treat it
with great reverence, almost like a person, getting it up in the
morning and putting it to bed at night, their attitude can verge
on idolatry.

Sikhism is not just a system of belief but also a way of life.
The social and religious are inextricably entwined. It does not
claim to be the only true religion but believes that all religions

originated with good intentions and are like different roads leading to the same destination. In its formation it rejected some aspects of Islam, such as the set times of prayer, the need for pilgrimage and the attitude to women. It also rejected the authority of the Hindu priests and scriptures, the practice of sacrifice, idol worship and the caste system. But Sikhism accepted some hymns and teaching from the Hindus and Muslims and today some moderate Sikh groups accept teaching from the New Testament. Generally they accept what they see as good in other religions. They regard Sikhism as one of many ways to God and consider it to be the simplest.

Christian witness

The claim of Christians that Christ is the only way to God, the only way of salvation, is an offence and a great stumbling block to the Sikh. When we are speaking with a Sikh we should not begin by saying that Jesus is the only way to God. This contradicts all they have been taught or imbibed from childhood and will almost certainly be the hardest doctrine for them to believe when they wish to become Christians.

If you visit Sikhs they will be very hospitable and friendly. Don't confuse this with an openness to the gospel. They will be very welcoming to you as a person but they are not longing for your 'good news' and they have no desire to change their religion. That is even more difficult for a Sikh than for a Hindu.

Not many Sikhs in Britain have become Christians as yet. Most of those who have believed in Jesus have done so because a Christian has spent a long time with them, listening to their needs, helping them practically, passing on a little of the faith at a time and praying for them. In some areas Asians are suffering the effects of unemployment. This is unfortunately leading to a rise in alcoholism, debt and marriage problems, including wife-beating. Sometimes a wife or a mother has come to Jesus because of the needs in her own life, the help of a Christian and the work of the Holy Spirit, but it has been a long process. Then in some cases the husband or the children have followed. As with other religious groups the more involved they are in their local religious community the harder it is for them to make the break and follow Christ.

Aspects of their faith that can act as a bridge to explaining Christian faith could include the teachings of Nanak. His belief that God is one and should alone be worshipped, provides common ground for us, as does his emphasis on the equality of all people and the ethical nature of worship.

We can also share the Sikh's respect for scriptures. It would be unthinkable to them to put their own scriptures on the floor, or mark then in any way; when we are with them it would be insensitive to treat our Bibles in a way which they would regard as disrespectful.

If we wish to help a Sikh colleague, neighbour or friend to believe in Jesus we must be willing to love them, spend time with them, show concern and win the opportunity to speak of Jesus. When they become Christians we must be willing to stand by them, discipling them and sharing fellowship with them because they will be rejected by their own community, and probably by their family and friends too.

Discussion starters

1. If you live in an Asian neighbourhood how would you know whether those you meet or visit are Sikhs? What is distinctive about their dress, their homes, their practices?

2. What particular problems are faced by Asians in your neighbourhood? How can you show your love for them in these situations?

3. In what ways will the beliefs of Sikhs vary from those of Muslims or Hindus?

4. Share any experience you have of meeting or knowing Sikhs. How far were their beliefs and practices orthodox, and to what extent had they assimilated to the local culture?

5. Re-read the Mool Mantra (p 81). Which statements do you think the Bible would agree with and which would its teaching reject?

6. Which Christian beliefs will be difficult for a Sikh to accept and which beliefs might be more attractive?

7. When you wish to share your faith with a Sikh what will it be helpful to remember?

Buddhism

Buddhism shares many basic ideas with Hinduism because it emerged in India from the same roots. They share the doctrines of karma (every action has its consequences, either good or bad, and that all bad actions must be compensated for) and of reincarnation, but in slightly different forms. In Hinduism it is the self which is reincarnated, while in Buddhism it is our karma which goes on from life to life; it is our good or bad works which have eternal consequences. Both religions share the same fundamental goal of Nirvana. But the character of Nirvana is somewhat different for each. In Hinduism it means that we sink into Brahman, while in Buddhism Nirvana is the indescribable state of neither being nor non-being. It is not a state of annihilation, but neither is it a place where we exist.

The Buddha

Many far-fetched myths surround the life story of Siddhartha Gautama, the Buddha or 'Enlightened One'. What we know is that he lived as the son of a wealthy king in North India and was brought up in the luxury of the palace. The exact dates of his life are uncertain. Some scholars say he was born in 623 BC, others claim 563 BC.

The turning point of his life came when he was twenty-nine years old. He rode out in his chariot from the palace and met the sufferings of the outside world. He saw a beggar, a funeral procession, a sick person and a weak old man. So he became aware of the sufferings of poverty, death, sickness and the decay of old age. On a later occasion he came across a monk, begging, but who was content with his way of life – even joyful.

And so came the Night of the Great Renunciation when the Buddha decided to leave the palace splendour and seek his salvation. Heavenly voices called to him, 'Go forth into the house-less state.' So he left his wife and son, and began a search for the way to freedom from the endless cycle of death and rebirth. He tried the Hindu way of asceticism and austerity, but this failed to give him the knowledge he wanted. Then he decided to try again the route of meditation which he had once practised. Eventually, after a prolonged period of meditation, he gained the understanding for which he had been looking.

At first he was reluctant to share his insights with others but, after he had preached his first sermon, five of his former disciples who heard it became the founding members of the first Buddhist monastic order. The Buddha then devoted his life to preaching the way of enlightenment to others.

There are two types of Buddhism, Theravada Buddhism and Mahayana Buddhism. Some scholars would also distinguish between Mahayana and its branch, Vajrayana, on the basis of the very different characteristics of each. A major distinctive of Vajrayana is its reliance on *tantra*, which we look at further on in the chapter.

THERAVADA BUDDHISM

This form of Buddhism is found in Sri Lanka, Burma, Thailand, Laos and Kampuchea. It is the mainstream and stricter form, but in practice is heavily infiltrated by traditional spiritism and animism. Almost every Thai home and factory, for example, will have an ornate spirit house outside where little offerings will be placed. The highly sophisticated and educated tour guide on a Bangkok coach said to us, 'Every Thai believes in the spirits.'

The main beliefs of Theravada Buddhism are expressed in the *Four Noble Truths* and the *Eightfold Path*.

The Four Noble Truths

As a result of his experience of enlightenment, the Buddha taught the following four truths.

1. *All is suffering*. 'Birth is suffering, sickness is suffering, death is suffering.'
2. *Desire or thirst causes suffering*. In particular it is the craving for existence which forms the basis of all suffering. Because we want to exist, we develop all sorts of emotions – love, hatred, hunger, sexual desire and so on. These desires for self-existence bring tension and suffering with them.
3. *Suffering ends when desire ends*. If we can get rid of all emotion – so losing all separate, individual existence – then we can be freed from suffering and from the chain of constant reincarnation.
4. *Freedom from suffering and being can be achieved*. The way to achieve this is to follow the 'Eightfold Path'.

The Eightfold Path

This is a description of the eight ways in which a person must discipline himself if he is to become fully detached from his desire for life. It is commonly called 'The Middle Way' because it steers a course between the two extremes of asceticism and self-indulgence.

1. *Right views*. The four truths given by Buddha are to be accepted and all contrary views rejected.
2. *Right resolve*. A man's resolve should be to aim for the highest goals – such as goodwill and peaceableness – and absence of all desire, lust and hatred.

3. *Right speech*. Speech is to be wise and truthful, never containing gossip or lies. It is always to be for a good purpose.
4. *Right conduct*. Murder, stealing and adultery are among the acts specifically prohibited for the Buddhist. He is to be charitable towards all people.
5. *Right livelihood*. A man must earn his living in an occupation that does no harm to others. He must not live a life of luxury.
6. *Right effort*. The Buddhist must be constantly making the effort to bar all evil desires from his mind and to develop and acquire inner virtues.
7. *Right awareness*. The aim is to have complete control of one's mental and physical processes, so one must become aware of them and of one's feelings.
8. *Right meditation*. This is the ability to concentrate the mind totally, in undivided attention.

The eight ways are really concerned with only three subjects: wisdom, morals and meditation. Through wisdom (right views, right resolve) one comes to know that 'a Self is not mine and what originates and perishes is but suffering'. By practising right morals (right speech, right conduct, right livelihood) a person gains enough merit to improve his karma. Eventually this may earn him the right to become an *Arhat*, someone who is ready for enlightenment. By meditation and trance (right effort, right awareness, right meditation) one is freed from existence.

This is obviously a highly complex and demanding system for achieving salvation by 'works'. One lifetime is not considered nearly long enough to master it all, and so the cycle of reincarnation plays a vital part, continuing until enlightenment is reached. In fact, this code of behaviour is primarily for monks and it is only as a monk that enlightenment can be attained. The layman seeks merit only in the hope of becoming a monk in his next incarnation.

In mainstream Buddhism the monks have great influence not only in religious teaching and practice, but also in agriculture and education. Strict rules govern the life of a monk.

Every morning they go from house to house with their begging bowl to get food for the day. They show no interest in what food is given to them and are not expected to thank their donor. The laity gain merit by giving food to them, so there is no reason for the monk to thank them.

Philosophy

The beliefs of Buddhism and the outworking of them in the Eightfold Path depend on two main principles: *anicca* or impermanence, and *anatha* or non-self.

Impermanence

In the constant chain of reincarnation we move from birth to growth to decay, and on to death. But death is not the end; 'all is a wheel of becoming' and after death comes another birth.

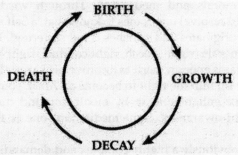

As nothing is permanent, lasting or has enduring value, one should not be concerned for anything or anyone. The Buddha, for example, stressed that it is better to be in the so-called 'house-less' state than to be attached to things. He also called his son Rahula, meaning 'a fetter', indicating that family connections merely tie us to existence and so to suffering. Life is only a bridge, so 'build no house upon it'.

The Christian will note that this teaching denies any sense of responsibility or stewardship, either for the created world or for one's own family. It also rules out any need for social concern. Buddhist philosophy denies the possibility of there being a creating and unchanging God. It is also quite specific in its rejection of the idea of the world having either beginning or end. Although the creation story in Genesis is radically contrary to Buddhist teaching, it may attract the Buddhist because of its simple description of how everything began. Some Buddhists are searching for an answer to the question, 'How did it all begin?'

Non-self

Buddhists have a story which helps explain this concept. One day the Buddha asked his disciple Ananda to bring him a chariot. As he pointed at the wheels, he asked:

'What are those, Ananda?'

'Wheels, master.'

'Remove them!'

He then pointed at the axle and asked, 'What is that, Ananda?'

'Axle, master.'

'Remove it!'

One bit of the chariot after another was removed in the same way until nothing was left.

'Where is the chariot?' the Buddha asked.

'There is no chariot, master.'

The various constituent parts appear to be there, but actually nothing really exists. The same applies to human life. Our hands, feet, head appear to be, but we are not – and if you strip them down, our hands, feet, head are not either.

In Hinduism only Brahman actually is. Everything else is an illusion. Buddhism would feel that this is a compromise. Actually nothing exists; even Brahman is an illusion. Nirvana is the ultimate extinction of being. It is often equated in Buddhist thought with *Sunyata*, the void, absolute emptiness. Suffering comes from the illusion that we exist. Release from suffering comes from being enlightened and realizing that we are not, that nothing is:

'Mere suffering exists, no sufferer is found;
The deed is, but no doer of the deed is there;
Nirvana is, but not the man that enters it;
The Path is, but no traveller on it is seen.'

MAHAYANA BUDDHISM

In practice it is hard to live in the light of strict Theravada
Buddhist philosophy. All of us need to live in a way that gives
some significance to life, to people and to the world around us.
In true Theravada Buddhist philosophy there can be no belief
in God or gods, no prayer and no worship. In practice, therefore, no one lives in true adherence to such beliefs. We have
already seen that in Thailand, for example, the vast majority of
people believe in spirits, and most daily religious practices
relate to them. People appease them with offerings and are
careful not to offend them. Temples abound and huge statues
of the Buddha unmistakably form the centre of worship and
prayer. Lay people will go to worship or meditate, and to be
instructed by the monks living on site. Their worship will
involve confession and the offering of flowers, light (candles)
and incense.

It is also unsatisfying to try to live a life where one avoids
all emotion and attempts to suppress all *tanha* or desire.
Underneath the cool and peaceful exterior of the Buddhist
there is often a suppressed violence which has built up
because their other emotions have had no outlet. A boiling
kettle needs an outlet for the steam.

The lack of concern for the world and for people also has sad
consequences. It can result in an uncaring lack of interest in the
welfare of other people. This is very noticeable in Thailand
with its rampant poverty and prostitution rackets. And leprosy
patients get little or no compassionate medical care.

Because of its extreme difficulty and impracticality,
Theravada Buddhism is followed by only a few Buddhists.
Another form of Buddhism has arisen which is less rigid in its
philosophy and warmer in its religious forms. Mahayana

Buddhism is followed by the majority of Buddhists and is found in Nepal, Tibet, Bhutan, Japan, Korea and among the Chinese.

Beliefs

Because Mahayana is a tolerant form of Buddhism, it always welcomes into its fabric the beliefs and practices of other religious systems. In Nepal, for example, it is mixed with the country's main religion, Hinduism. So there are as many beliefs and philosophies in Mahayana Buddhism as there are groups of people who practise it. We will look at three of these in more detail below: Zen, and the practices of yoga and tantrism.

In general, however, Mahayana places less emphasis than Theravada on the eradication of desire as the means to enlightenment. Rather it teaches that the Buddha spirit is in every person. Through transcendent wisdom (*Prajna*) and right living one can develop this Buddha spirit to perfection eventually becoming a full Buddha. This is what Siddhartha Gautama did, developing his Buddha spirit to perfection, by accumulating good karma during many reincarnations.

The final stage before actually becoming a Buddha is that of a *Boddhisatva*. The Buddha himself temporarily renounced enlightenment in order to help other people set their feet on the path of Buddhism. Others too, en route to Buddhahood, will pass through that stage of near-enlightenment as a Boddhisatva.

In Theravada Buddhism each individual must seek their own salvation without looking for help from anyone else, even from the Buddha. But Mahayana Buddhism allows prayer to the Buddha and the Boddhisatvas.

Zen

Zen Buddhism developed with the Mahayana branch of Buddhism. It has spread widely from its origins in Japan to become influential in many Western countries. It is the expression of Buddhism which probably has most appeal to Westerners, emphasizing meditation and detachment from the world over against the frenetic activism of much Western life.

There are two stories which tell of the origin of Zen. It is said that a man came to the Buddha, asking him to preach to him the way of enlightenment. He offered Buddha a flower made of gold in payment. The Buddha took the flower and gazed at it, gazed at it and continued to gaze at it. Finally the man smiled; and this smile is the origin of Zen.

Another story tells of a man who was meditating at length. The Buddha asked him, 'Why do you meditate?' The man answered, 'I want to become a Buddha.' The Buddha then took a brick and began to polish it. He polished it for a long time until the man eventually smiled. This smile, too, is the origin of Zen.

What do these stories teach? The first, that meditation offers a way of enlightenment, whereas preaching with its multitude of words will not be able to. But then the second story shows that meditation too may not succeed. It is impossible to polish a brick – with all the rubbing in the world it will never shine. Even meditation is in itself inadequate. There are no means to enlightenment which really suffice.

What, then, does Zen teach? The leading British Buddhist, Christmas Humphreys, says that Zen Buddhism achieves enlightenment through non-sense (not nonsense!). Zen aims to take a person beyond the realm of sense – beyond what we know, feel, think, or see; beyond any particular means to enlightenment. Enlightenment can be gained instantaneously by a sudden, intuitive grasp of the truth, perhaps when meditating on paradoxical sayings. Zen does not teach that enlightenment will always take a number of reincarnations to achieve.

The key to understanding Zen is the statement, 'A crane's legs are long; a duck's legs are short.' What is, is right. Don't try to change things. Don't struggle against what you consider to be evil. Learn to accept that cranes just do have long legs and ducks have short ones. Quiet acceptance without the tension of striving or desire may be the prelude to enlightenment.

Buddhist practices

Yoga

This has its origins in Hinduism, and is a philosophy rather than simply a system of exercises. The word *yoga* comes from a term meaning a yoke, the implication being that a person should yoke his mind with total concentration to one object until he obtains release from all self-awareness. Through such concentration he may escape from the 'five hindrances' to enlightenment: longing for existence, malice, laziness, distraction and doubt. So he enters into a growing experience of trance with levitation, leading to the 'three knowledges': knowing his former incarnations, knowing the path of reincarnation, and knowing the destruction of desire and ignorance.

Yoga may be practised by means of concentrated meditation or by means of physical exercises designed to liberate the practitioner from all awareness of himself or the world around him. The meditation may be on a short sentence (maybe a word) which is repeated constantly until he loses conscious awareness of life.

As Christians we may notice the danger of all practices which lead us to lose awareness of our surroundings or of ourselves. It is highly dangerous to say or sing something so often that one enters into a sort of trance state. Emptying the mind allows demonic powers to fill the vacuum.

Tantrism

Tantric Buddhism seems to have come from Hindu influence around the middle of the first Christian millennium. It emphasizes the use of ritual and sacred formulas, with occult practices, as a short-cut to Nirvana. Central to these activities is a magical symbolic design, called a mandala, which may be drawn or painted, but may also be represented in the shape of a temple(e.g. Borobodur in Java, Indonesia). Through trance, the tantric Buddhist aims to achieve unity with the Buddha who will appear to him with other supernatural beings around him.

Tantrism is particularly found in Tibet and Mongolia, but its magical and occult practices are becoming increasingly popular among Western young people. Yoga is often the first step towards the deeper use of trance and spiritism in Tantrism.

Meditation

Both Theravada and Mahayana Buddhism encourage the use of meditation. So do Hinduism and Christianity. But we need to be careful to define what we mean by meditation. Each religion uses it in a different way.

A Hindu meditates on something with the aim of losing self-consciousness, for he does not believe that he actually exists. He is also to lose consciousness of what he is meditating on, for that too is really an illusion. The only true reality is Brahman, so he aims to sink through meditation into the great ocean of Brahman. Everything else ceases to be. The meditator is not. What he meditates on is not. Only Brahman is.

Buddhism is similar, but more radical. Here too, the Buddhist will lose consciousness both of himself and also of the object of his meditation. But he is not trying to sink like a drop of water into the great ocean of Brahman, for Brahman also is not. His aim is so to meditate that all becomes a blank, a vacuum (*sunyata*). Nothing is.

Christian meditation is totally different. We believe that God exists and that he has created both us and the world around us. The Christian does not meditate in order to escape from what God has created; meditation on some thing or on particular words, is done in order to learn something of God from it. In Christian meditation verbal formulas are not repeated so that we lose consciousness of what we are saying or turn our minds into an empty blank. The Christian meditates on the nature and actions of God himself. We do not lose consciousness of ourselves, rather we see ourselves more clearly as we begin to understand how God sees us.

Christian witness

The key to Christian witness among Buddhists and Hindus remains the foundational truth that God is, and that Jesus also is the 'I am'. From this truth we deduce that as individuals we have tremendous significance because God created us and we bear his image. The world, too, is his creation and has real importance. As a result, peace and salvation are to be found in the world and in relationship to others, not by release from all awareness of our surroundings and neighbours. Life becomes so significant that the Christian promise of salvation is in fact 'eternal life': a wonderful promise, not a fearful threat.

Discussion Starters

1. What did the Buddha say causes suffering, and what solution to it did he teach? How does this compare with the Bible's teaching about the Fall of mankind and the death of Christ? (See, for instance, Genesis 1:26-31; 3:1-24; Isaiah 53:16; Romans 8:1-4 and 35-39; Revelation 21:1-4.)

2. 'Life is only a bridge, so build no house upon it' (p 92). As a Christian, how could you agree with a Buddhist here? Where would you have to disagree and why?

3. How do you react to the story about Ananda and the chariot (p 93)? What point does it make and how would you reply to it as a Christian?

4. What could you say to a Buddhist, and what could you do, to show him that he has enormous personal worth?

5. What differences are there in aims and method between Buddhist meditation and Christian meditation?

6. How important are the emotions and the mind in Buddhism and in Christianity? How would you explain Jesus' words in Matthew 22:36-39 to a Buddhist?

8

Traditional Chinese and Japanese religions

We have already noted that Mahayana Buddhism tolerates, and so merges with, other religions. No one can call themselves a 'pure' Mahayana Buddhist. Traditional Chinese religion fuses Confucianism and Taoism with Buddhism; traditional Japanese religion fuses Confucianism and Shinto with Buddhism. Because of this, Japanese or Chinese Buddhists might hardly recognize the previous chapter's description of Buddhism as being the religion they practise.

```
                  BUDDHISM
                      +
                CONFUCIANISM
           +                  +
        TAOISM              SHINTO
          ↓                   ↓
      Traditional         Traditional
        Chinese             Japanese
        religion            religion
```

TRADITIONAL CHINESE RELIGION

The temple worship of the Chinese is generally Buddhist in form (although the temple idols are not statues of Buddha but of traditional spirits or deities from ancient Chinese myth).

Their popular religion – in the home and in birth, marriage and death ceremonies – is Taoist, and their ethics, social relationships and practical living are Confucian.

Confucianism

Confucius (K'ung Fu-Tzu) was born in about 551 BC during a time of fearful corruption and political despotism. Much of his teaching therefore concentrates on finding answers to the problems these things threw up. How can a society live in a right way? He knew the bitterness of social disorder and political oppression. It is said that he met a woman weeping because her father, her husband and her only son had all been eaten by a tiger. Confucius asked her why she continued to live in such a dangerous place. 'It is the only place without an oppressive ruler,' she replied. Her reply illustrates Confucius' teaching that it is better to suffer the loss of loved ones than to live in an unjust society.

Confucius himself died without having achieved much. Tradition affirms that his dying words were, 'No intelligent ruler takes me as his master!' But through his followers, particularly the great Mencius in the fourth century BC, his teachings became highly influential in China and remained so for many centuries. From the Middle Ages until the revolution of 1900 all Chinese civil servants had to pass exams in the Confucian classics in order to gain promotion. The two most significant books were *The Book of Changes* and *The Analects*, the latter being a collection of Confucius' sayings.

Beliefs and practice

There are four foundations to Confucianist ethics and belief.

1. *The Way (the Tao)*
   Confucius refused to discuss religious questions that did not directly affect life in society now. 'If you don't understand this life, how can I tell you of the after-life?' he asked.

But he did encourage the continuation of religious practices in order to hold society together. The climax of these practices was the Emperor's annual ritual sacrifice to Heaven. 'Heaven' cannot be equated with God, however, for it is remote and impersonal: 'Heaven does not speak'. The Tao is the word used to describe 'The Way of Heaven', and the person who follows the decrees of Heaven is following the Tao. This Way is defined in the other three foundational teachings:

2. *Love (Ren) and Righteousness or truth (I)*
Confucius' concern was that society should be well ordered, peaceful and 'respectful'. He believed that man was fundamentally good and could bring about this sort of society if he observed the 'Five Relationships' and the 'Five Constants'. The whole stability of society depends on five relationships: the prince and his minister; the father and his son; the husband and his wife; the elder brother and the younger brother; friend with friend. In traditional Chinese thought the first four are between a superior and the one under him, while the two friends are equals. It is in the context of these relationships that Confucius gave the well-known Golden Rule, 'Don't do to others what you would not desire them to do to you.' The Christian will notice that this Golden Rule lacks the positive note of Jesus', 'Love your neighbour as yourself' (Mark 12:31). Within these five stable relationships, the Confucian is to practise the Five Constants of moral behaviour: kindness, justice, reverence, wisdom and loyalty.

3. *Loyalty*
Confucianism underlines the last of the Five Constants. In social relationships, submissive obedience and service by the inferior must be matched by the wise and good example of the superior who senses his responsibility towards his inferior. We are to show loyalty unto death for our prince, parent, husband or older brother. Likewise our teacher stands above us and demands our loyalty. This is

the cement which keeps society whole. Unselfishness in community relationships brings cohesion and unity.

If, as Christians, we are to have an attractive witness in Chinese circles, we shall need to demonstrate loving relationships which will include loyal respect for those above us, particularly our parents, older relations and teachers.

4. *Ritual*

External rituals express the reality of our loyal relationships. For example, we show our respect for our ancestors by making the right offerings to them. Life consists of a multitude of externals each of which will demonstrate a right attitude. Good manners are therefore very important in Chinese society. We in Europe are very casual today in such matters and will need to learn much greater care in the niceties of behaviour if we are to relate well in Chinese society.

However, these externals carry with them the danger of meaningless formalism which becomes just an empty tradition. This is one reason why many young, educated Chinese rebel against traditional Chinese ways and can be very open to the Christian faith. Although Confucius rejected mere rote learning, saying that 'to learn and not to think over is useless', in practice Confucianism has not given reasons for its external forms.

The main religious ritual is still the practice of ancestor veneration. Food and prayers are offered to the dead and this is today the greatest obstacle preventing Confucians from becoming Christians. Mendcis said that 'the chief evil is to die without a son to serve the family altar'. Chinese Christians struggle with the New Testament teaching about food offered to spirits, wanting to show filial respect and family loyalty without performing such rituals.

Taoism

Taoism is said to have been founded by Lao Tzu, the traditional author of the well-known Chinese classic, the *Tao Te*

Ching. The Tao Te Ching may well date from around the fourth century BC, but scholars are unsure as to whether Lao Tzu ever actually existed. In any case the teachings of Taoism developed largely through the later disciple of Lao Tzu called Chuang Tzu (born in 330 BC). As so often with Asian religions, it is not the historical reality of the founders which is important, but rather their ideas. Taoism has four main elements:

Tao

Whereas Confucianism sees Tao as the Way of Heaven, Taoism regards it as the first principle behind the whole order of nature. Man follows the laws of Heaven, but Heaven follows the laws of Tao. Tao is therefore the universal principle, the way of nature. Man's aim in life is to follow this Tao, with the aim of living in a state of perfect harmony with unspoilt nature.

Virtue (Te)

Te, or virtue, is the discarding of all selfishness and artificiality in one's conduct, in order to return to the simple life of nature.

Submission (Wu Wei)

Te is practised by a passive submission to the Tao, which is called *Wu Wei*. It is said that there was a man who ran hard to escape from his own shadow and from the sound of his footsteps. The harder he ran, the more his shadow followed him and the louder his footsteps sounded. The moral? Be still under the shadow of a tree! Relax and submit to the natural order. This is the passivity of Wu Wei and the virtue of Te.

Taoism looks back to the golden age of the ancient, perhaps mythical, Chou Dynasty of China. Since then human beings have lost their primitive, natural innocence through so-called wisdom, education and civilization. Governments and laws interfere with our natural instincts. Effort takes us away from the Tao. Learning and education cause us to leave our natural purity. It is said, 'You cannot speak of the ocean to a well-frog or of ice to a summer insect. You cannot speak of Tao to an academic – his scope is too restricted.'

In Taoist-influenced Chinese paintings, human figures merge discreetly into the background, and the representations of nature are drawn with shaded lines, not with bold outlines. By contrast, in Western painting the human or animal figures stand out starkly against their natural backgrounds. In Taoist painting there must be no stark contrasts, but rather a quiet merging.

The harmony of opposites (Yin/Yang)
The Tao consists of the harmony of the opposites which govern the universe. Everything has its opposite: *Yin* represents femininity, earth, cold, passivity, darkness and death; *yang* is masculinity, heaven, hot, active, light, life. But rather than standing over against each other, they fuse into each other: the male relates to the female, heaven to earth, hot to cold, passive to active, and so on.

In the diagram we see that the light and dark merge with gentle curves, they do not stand with hard straight lines against each other. And there is a light area in the dark section and a dark area in the light section: that is the harmony of the Tao.

But the concept of Yin and Yang has also been used in Taoism for occult purposes. The Yin of in-breathing and the Yang of out-breathing gives rise to such concentration on one's breathing that all awareness of one's self evaporates. The resultant mental emptiness leads easily to spirit-filling. Discerning the lucky or favourable Yin as opposed to the unfavourable Yang requires the services of the Taoist priest and his spiritualistic practices. He would, for instance, discern what date is favourable for a wedding. This is linked, too, to the mystical use of particular diagramatic pictures. Taoism came to stress China's magical heritage; today it is still the practice of Taoism which provides an entry for spiritism.

One writer has said, 'the very essence of Taoism is the search after immortality'. The Yin of Hell and the Yang of Heaven are vivid realities in the minds of the Chinese. I remember my first visit to the Tiger Balm gardens in Singapore. The huge stone representations of the tortures and agonies of hell force themselves upon you. Demons tear out the tongues of sinners. Fire licks away the flesh of men and women. Horrific scenes of this type make hell such a reality that many Chinese are drawn to faith in Christ because he offers salvation from it.

In the afterlife it is believed that we shall use money, houses and cars just as we do in this world. So at a Taoist funeral it is customary to burn paper money and other paper objects in order to ensure that the departed spirit will have ample in the afterlife. There are similarities here with the practice of ancestor worship in Confucianism.

To summarize Chinese religion: Taoism satisfies the human need of colourful ritual with a definite sense of spiritual realities, Buddhism adds its deeper philosophy, while Confucianism brings its ethics, community structures and morals in relationships. Together they form a significant religious approach. However, under the pressure of modern education and the desire for material progress, Chinese religion fails to satisfy. The door is wide open for Christian witness among the Chinese and many are becoming Christians. Large and dynamic Chinese churches thrive all over the world.

TRADITIONAL JAPANESE RELIGION

Traditional Chinese and traditional Japanese religion are both founded on Buddhism. Confucianism determines the social dimension of each, giving them their dynamism and efficiency. But instead of Taoism the Japanese have traditional

Shintoism and, more recently, they have added new religions based on a type of Buddhism.

Shintoism

The Japanese tea ceremony, the cherry blossom festival, Mount Fuji's perfection with its snow-capped cone, shrines or temples surrounded by gardens with wooden bridges over water – harmony and simplicity in nature underlie the religion of Shintoism.

Shinto teaches that the perfection of nature is seen particularly in the land of Japan. When the gods created the world, the process began when their footprints formed the islands of Japan. Only then did the creative power of the gods flow from Japan to make the rest of the world. Nationalism is at the very heart of the Shinto tradition.

Prior to the Second World War the emperors of Japan were considered to be the descendants of the gods, and therefore divine. From the emperors came the chief priests of Shinto and through them the lesser priests too. This gives the Shinto religion a divine mandate which, together with a religiously based nationalism, gave rise to the militancy of the Second World War. The eighteenth-century leader Moto-Ori, and his disciple Hirata, spelt out that the Japanese emperor, land and people were unique and should rule the world. Likewise they taught that because the Japanese are related to the gods they are naturally good. If the Japanese would merely follow their natural instincts, all would be well. Corruption, they taught, comes from outside, from foreign influences. It was Shinto teaching, therefore, that led to Japan becoming a closed land where no foreign contact was permitted for several centuries.

The nationalistic emphasis is particularly seen in the sect of Shinto called State or Shrine Shinto. In this movement worship is centred on certain shrines – to the sun goddess Amaterasu, to the spirits of ancestral heroes, or to ancestors and emperors. Here the war dead are also honoured. The main shrine is at Ise.

The world of Shinto is peopled by a multitude of *Kami*, spirits or gods. These not only indwell emperors and special ancestral figures but also the shrines themselves and a host of natural objects of beauty or special note. Mount Fuji itself, trees of unusual shape and rivers may all be the special homes of Kami. The second great movement of Shinto, *Sectarian Shinto*, centres its worship on this multitude of Kami within nature. Sectarian Shinto relates closely to the traditional Japanese love of nature, stressing the sense of harmony with the environment.

NEW JAPANESE RELIGIOUS MOVEMENTS

After the Second World War the Western armies compelled the Japanese Emperor to declare publicly that he was not divine. This, combined with the shattering realization that the powers of Shinto and Japan had been defeated, led to grave religious questionings by many Japanese. Japan hovered in a spiritual vacuum. But although they admired Christianity, the people were not prepared to accept a foreign religion.

A great variety of new religious movements based on Nichiren Buddhism then swarmed into this vacuum. Nichiren (1222-1282) was a Buddhist Japanese nationalist who had stressed that religion and national life should be one. He taught that in the last days the seat of the Buddha would be established in Japan and from Japan would flow the saving teaching of Buddhahood. In preparation for this the Law of Japan and the Law of Buddha should be one. With regard to religion he emphasized the Buddhist scripture known as the Lotus Sutra, and taught that the use of any other scriptures is both unnecessary and bad.

It is from these Nichiren roots that the new religious movements of Soka Gakkai, Tenrikyo and many others have now sprung up. In fewer than twenty years after the end of the war, 171 official new religious movements were registered with twenty per cent of the Japanese being members of them. The largest and most dynamic is Soka Gakkai.

Soka Gakkai

This movement promises enlightenment and salvation from
constant reincarnation, as well as prosperity here on earth. Its
first post-war president, Toda Josei, taught that man needs to
'be healthy, have money and have peace in his home'. If there
is no evidence of material blessing now, what evidence is there
of Buddhahood after death? One Soka Gakkai temple therefore has an advertisement outside which reads:

> Rewards for belief:
> healing from sickness, harmony in the home, business success,
> safety at sea, protection from travel accidents.

Great emphasis is placed on faith healings and other miracles
through the power of the Soka Gakkai mandate, a graphic pic-
torial representation of the universe with the Eternal Buddha
at the centre and other Buddhas around and below following
the order described in the Lotus Sutra. Through this mandala
death itself is overcome, the sign of which is that the corpse
becomes soft and light like cotton.

The appeal of Soka Gakkai seems to come largely through
its worship where large crowds are brought together. This in
itself engenders quite an atmosphere. The services consist of
three sections. Firstly, the crowd unite in the constant repetition of a set prayer called the *Daimoku*; this goes on for about
twenty minutes. Then the Lotus Sutra is recited for a further
twenty minutes. Finally there is another twenty minutes for
more repetition of the Daimoku.

In the central temple of Soka Gakkai, homage is also paid to
the tooth of Nichiren. It is said that the flesh of the gums is
growing up around the tooth and is now nearly covering it.
When the flesh finally covers the whole tooth, that will be the
climax of the growth of Soka Gakkai and of world history.

Soka Gakkai has given birth to a political wing, the *Clean
State Party*, which has become a significant force in parliament.
The movement also developed the doctrine of *Shakufuku*,
'break and subdue'. The post-war president of the Soka

Gakkai Party encouraged his followers to 'exterminate all false religions' and their *Handbook for Teaching Converts* ridicules works of service to humanity, stressing rather the work of winning others to become converts to Soka Gakkai.

Christian witness

What are the keys to Christian witness among the Chinese and Japanese? Firstly, our spiritual vitality needs to be apparent, as well as our cultivation of loving relationships in our homes and in society.

Secondly, we will need to demonstrate good moral standards and an intelligent use of our minds, as the Confucian background stresses the importance of education and learning as the foundation for right living within society.

Thirdly, the Taoist and Shinto backgrounds encourage people to be in touch with spiritual realities, so the Christian will need to demonstrate his or her personal knowledge of God. Their strong emphasis on the demonic spirit world means that we shall need to be particularly aware of occult powers. We can also assure people with this background that in Jesus Christ we have a loving power which can overcome any demonic force.

Discussion starters

1. What does the command, 'Honour your father and your
   mother' mean (Exodus 20:12)? What is the difference
   between this and the worship of dead parents or grandparents?

2. Look again at the 'Five Relationships' and the 'Five
   Constants' of Confucianism (p 103). How far could a
   Christian Chinese person affirm these? Where would he or
   she need to add to them or even contradict them? Why?

3. How significant are external rituals and forms of worship to
   the Confucian? How would you explain the Bible's teaching about worship to such a person? (Compare, for
   instance, Amos 5:21-24; Micah 6:8 and Matthew 6:1-8; with
   Matthew 25:31-36 and James 2:14-16.)

4. What rituals do we have in our worship which we now
   keep up only for the sake of tradition? Should we abandon
   them? Why or why not?

5. 'The Tao consists of the harmony of opposites which govern
   the universe' (p 106). How would you contrast this with the
   Bible's teaching on good and evil? What are the dangers of
   the Taoist view?

6. 'Nationalism is at the very heart of the Shinto tradition'
   (p 108). Why is this? What is at the heart of the Christian
   faith? How does this affect our view of nationalism?

7. Look again at the advertisement displayed outside one
   Soka Gakkai temple (p 110). How would you reply to a
   member of the Soka Gakkai movement who said that your
   faith in the Christian God was obviously wrong because he
   was not rewarding you with material success?

PART II

New Eastern Religious Movements

Introduction

During the 1960s many young people in the Western world became disenchanted with the materialism and secularism of post-war society. In their idealism they began to search for spiritual values. Many rejected the institutional churches and found their answer in groups like the Children of God and the Unification Church. Others of the hippy era travelled to the East, especially to India and Afghanistan, to seek new values and new ideas along with easier access to drugs. There many attached themselves to the gurus of Hinduism. As the disillusionment of Western youth became more apparent, some of the gurus travelled to North America and Europe spreading their teaching. A few, like Swami Prabhupada of the Hare Krishna movement and Maharashi Mahesh Yogi of Transcendental Meditation, were successful in building up large followings. Others, like Maharaj Ji of the Divine Light Mission, and the Indian guru Bhagwan Rajneesh, built up a strong following for some time and then were discredited. It is always possible that they will become significant groups again, so they should not be forgotten or ignored.

When studying new Eastern religious movements it is helpful to have an understanding of Hinduism. The highest philosophy of Hinduism is monistic (see chapter 5), believing that Brahman is the ultimate reality, the only reality and that all else is illusion. Transcendental Meditation is a modernized form of that stream of Hinduism. More popular in Hinduism is *Bhakti*, the religion of devotion, where a personal form or forms of Brahman can be worshipped. Generally this leads to polytheism, the worship of many gods. But one group of Hindus give the appearance of being monotheists, worshipping Krishna as the supreme incarnation of God. They are more accurately henotheists because they worship one god without maintaining that he is the only one. The Hare Krishna movement is a modern descendant of this group.

9

Krishna Consciousness, Osho: the Science of Meditation (Rajneeshism)

KRISHNA CONSCIOUSNESS

In the 1970s you might have seen shaven-headed, orange-robed young men in London's Oxford Street or other town centres in Britain, Europe or North America. They offered their magazine, *Back to Godhead*, or books or records, free and then asked for a donation. Today they still raise money and propagate their beliefs in the same way but are usually dressed more casually in jeans and tee shirts or sweaters, wearing wigs over their shaved heads. The group became well known in the 1960s when it enjoyed the support of one of the Beatles, George Harrison.

Origins

The correct name of the group is the International Society for Krishna Consciousness or ISKCON for short. Because of their practice of repeatedly reciting 'Hare Krishna' they are more commonly known as the Hare Krishna Movement. *Hare* means 'Lord' and *Krishna* is the name of that lord or Hindu god which they worship.

This movement follows teaching which originated in North India in the sixteenth century based on the Hindu scripture, the Bhagavadgita. It is marked by its worship and devotion to

Lord Krishna and the public chanting of the Hare Krishna
mantra or prayer chant. The guru who brought this teaching
from India to the West and founded ISKCON was A.C.
Bhakdivedanta Swami Prabhupada. In the 1930s his own guru
had told him to spread his message to the West but it was not
until he was seventy in 1965 that a wealthy Indian ship owner
gave him a berth on one of her ships going to America. On
reaching New York he began by sitting in Greenwich Village
chanting his mantra,

Hare Krishna, Hare Krishna,
Krishna, Krishna, Hare Hare,
Hare Rama, Hare Rama
Rama Rama, Hare Hare.

He had already translated much of his teaching into English
and soon the saffron-robed Indian teacher attracted young
people who had given up on the materialism of American
society and become hippies. In the hippie movement they had
found freedom and, in the drug culture, had gained 'religious
experiences'. But they had also discovered the evil effects of
drugs and many wanted a more coherent philosophy and purpose for life.

At this point Prabhupada arrived on the scene and
offered worship of Krishna in a disciplined community of
like-minded individuals. It appealed to disillusioned dropouts in a way it never did to young employed people. In the
late sixties and early seventies many joined the movement
not only in the USA but in other Western countries. Towards
the end of the 1970s and into the 1980s, when finding
employment became more difficult and therefore more
important to young people, the group's appeal lessened and
the organization seemed dated. However, at the beginning
of the twenty-first century it is encouraging people to worship Krishna in their homes with their families. Their website tells possible followers how to practise their devotions
and how to prepare and cook the special food to offer their
Lord Krishna. Temple devotees are willing to visit homes,

demonstrate congregational chanting and worship, and teach from their founder's books, not only for the family but also for any invited neighbours.

By 1977 when Swami Prabhupada died there were about seventy centres, 10,000 devotees in the USA, just under 1000 in Britain, and about 15,000 in the major cities of the rest of the Western world. The monthly magazine *Back to Godhead* was selling 300,000 copies of each issue, and a large incense factory in Los Angeles supplied finance and employment for the group.

After the guru's death twelve senior disciples were made 'gurus' worldwide but it was felt that the supreme guru should be an Indian. In 1982 Shri Sopal Krishna Maharaj was appointed leader but he was never more than a figurehead. At the same time twenty-five Governing Body Commissioners were also appointed to administer the organization with its huge finances and they attempted to control affairs from behind the scenes. Despite the fact that many of the other eleven 'gurus' have been dismissed because of serious misconduct there is still a power struggle for the position of the authoritative head of the organization, the single supreme guru.

For many years ISKCON did not appeal in India itself but during the 1980s it began to find favour among wealthy Indians who were willing to pay a life subscription to belong. They have access to a huge temple and to residential and cultural centres in Delhi and Bombay. They have four-star hotel service and good vegetarian restaurants in many Indian cities and other business centres in the world. At Mayapur in Bengal, India, the society is building a spiritual town devoted to Krishna worship with a temple, research centre, university, planetarium, theme park and guest facilities. This attracts many Indians as well as visitors from overseas.

In England the society originally appealed to young white British, but from the 1980s the Krishna temple in Letchmore Heath, Hertfordshire, began to serve as a worship centre for many Hindu Indians from north London.

Teaching

This group worships Krishna, not just as one of the incarnations of Vishnu, but as the supreme incarnation, the Lord, the Absolute Truth. The individual member is expected to show a personal, loving devotion to Krishna. An action is bound to be good if it is done out of love for Krishna; it is bad if it is not. Anyone who is truly Krishna conscious need fear no punishment; he has no bad karma.

Prabhupada taught that the soul of man is eternal and will be reborn into another body according to how a person has lived in this life. He also taught the unreality of the rest of the physical world. Attachment to family and job shows that the person is captivated by the material world; a devotee needs to give up such claims to know a true spiritual relationship with the Lord. If he lives in close Krishna consciousness he will not be reborn as an animal or as another human being but he will be transferred to Krishnaloka, the highest spiritual planet and personal abode of Krishna. So salvation lies in true devotion to Krishna. All actions should be done for him and then they cannot be bad for he is above good and evil.

His teaching led young people to give up their jobs, leave their families and devote themselves to the worship and service of Krishna. There are Krishna temples in many cities of the world. Devotees live in the temples under the authority of the temple President. In the temples are statues of gods – incarnations in material form of Krishna – which the devotees dust, dress, feed and bathe every morning.

Cleanliness is very important. A follower will begin the day at three in the morning with a shower and will take many more through the day, especially when he returns to the temple. His day is closely planned with periods for private chanting of mantras, services, study hours, chores and raising money on the streets. Only five or six hours sleep are allowed and there is almost no free time.

No alcohol, tobacco, tea, coffee, eggs, meat or fish are allowed and drugs can only be used on medical advice. Simple, Indian-style clothes are to be worn and devotees' heads are shaved apart from a plait or pigtail (which is left to symbolize their hope that Krishna will pull them up to heaven). Time is not to be wasted in sport, gambling or idle conversation. The followers' time should be spent in devotion to Krishna or encouraging others to worship him. Sexual relations outside marriage are forbidden and within marriage only once a month for the purpose of procreation. A husband should encourage his family's devotion but if the burden of family life distracts him from obtaining true Krishna consciousness, he should feel free to abandon family life. Women are considered inferior to men, less intelligent, and untrustworthy.

To become a member of the movement a follower must take part in temple life for six months and study the movement's teaching. Then there is an initiation ceremony by the temple President where the follower is given a new spiritual Sanskrit name and three strands of neck beads which he must wear all his life. After another six months the faithful are given a secret mantra to chant three times a day and men receive the sacred thread to wear over their shoulder and across their chest. The final ceremony is only for the special devotees who make a lifelong vow of poverty, celibacy and commitment to preaching and good works.

Krishna Consciousness and Christianity

At first sight there may seem to be many likenesses to Christianity. Followers of Krishna believe in one Lord to whom they commit their lives in personal devotion. They believe God is distinct from man and they understand salvation in terms of a personal relationship with a personal god. Devotees trying to influence Westerners will often stress that the differences are only a matter of terminology.

This is far from true. Christians will need to explain politely and respectfully the many significant differences. The Hare Krishnas believe in many gods of whom the most important is the Hindu god, Krishna, and they worship statues or idols of their god. They teach that Jesus was not God but a devotee of Krishna. This obviously contrasts with Christian belief in one God alone, a triune God of three persons – Father, Son and Holy Spirit.

Christian belief is based on the Bible whereas the followers of Krishna claim that the Bible has been distorted and reinterpreted in translation. Their authority is the Swami Prabhupada's interpretation of the Hindu scriptures, especially the Bhagavadgita.

Followers of Krishna believe that the material world is an illusion and has no importance, whereas Christians believe that God created the material world, is concerned about it and sent his Son to be born into it.

Krishna is a god who had many sexual adventures and is a cheat, whereas the God of the Bible is holy, righteous and without sin. Because of the amoral character of their god, followers of Krishna do not believe that deeds are good or evil in a moral sense. Anything is good if it is done for Krishna.

The belief that a person's soul is re-born into another body according to how he lives this life is also contrary to Christian belief. The New Testament teaches that salvation is gained by faith in Jesus Christ who has already taken the punishment for the sin of mankind. The Krishna movement teaches that it is gained only by the development of Krishna consciousness.

This movement originally proved attractive to idealistic young people who wished for a faith or organization to which they could give total commitment. Many of them came from agnostic or nominal Christian homes where they had not seen Christianity as a religion which expected absolute commitment to the Lordship of Christ. Now many wealthy Indians are associating with the group as an Englishman might belong to the parish church, the Rotary Club, Round Table or the Freemasons.

OSHO: THE SCIENCE OF MEDITATION (RAJNEESHISM)

Bhagwan Rajneesh was an Indian guru who, after teaching philosophy at university level in India, resigned his post in

1967 to consecrate his life to 'the spiritual regeneration of humanity, to spread practical spirituality for every man'. After making his headquarters in Bombay for a time he moved to Pune where he established a commune. During the six years he was there he gained many followers, mainly wealthy young people who had dropped out of Indian and Western society to join him. He only worked among the rich because he said that the materially poor could never be spiritual!

Although an able intellectual himself, his teaching was avowedly anti-intellectual. He taught that personal satisfaction and enlightenment was not to be found through reason, but through freedom from restrictions, through an emotional trip. He also used a complex set of techniques to de-condition the emotions. The 'dynamic' meditation he advocated involved violent movement, chaotic breathing and shaking of the body in order to attain a euphoric state which he termed enlightenment. The sign over the door of the Pune headquarters reads, 'Shoes and minds are to be left here at the gate.' As in tantric yoga sex was seen as a special way of experiencing the ultimate oneness of the universe and so free love was encouraged. There was some change in teaching and practice after the publicity about herpes and AIDS. Now outside the commune in India there are notices advertising it as an HIV-free zone.

In 1981 Rajneesh left Pune to found a new colony in Oregon, USA. He said that he did not want to create a new religion or cult but wanted to establish a new society, a 'New Age City'. After the disaster of Jonestown in Guyana in 1978 he advocated a totally different style of commune from the fanatical and self-sacrificing one established by Jones. It was to be a utopian society in which people had all the freedom they wanted and every modern convenience. Rajneesh became a wealthy millionaire many times over with more than ninety Rolls Royces and a colony protected by his own armed security service. When some of his followers were being investigated about offences against American immigration laws, he fled Oregon in his private jet. He tried to settle in the UK, Eire and South America, but in 1987 he returned to India. The Pune authorities allowed him to return because the commune and its many visitors provide a good income and tourist attraction.

When Rajneesh first began his community the only rule was that everyone should wear orange clothes but even that rule was rescinded. In Pune they now wear maroon robes to disassociate themselves from some of the excesses and bad publicity of the past. The movement's name was also changed to Osho: the Science of Meditation.

Rajneesh died in 1989 but his followers still revere him as the Enlightened One, who was Divinity personified and who has become one with the Infinite: the Cosmic Consciousness. They now speak of him as Osho and sell the books and tapes of his teaching. They remain anti-intellectual, advertising gibberish as a 'scientific' way to clear the mind. At a New Age Festival they were teaching deep stomach laughter as another way to find happiness and relieve tension. They now advocate different types of meditation as well as the dynamic one to relieve the stress of the twenty-first century – more gentle ones, including gazing at candles and dancing. The influence of Zen Buddhism is evident in their books, tapes, horoscopes and Tarot cards. Like other New Age groups they do not count membership, but over 35 years hundreds of thousands of people have been drawn to them from the wealthier nations of the world.

Christian witness

When getting to know people from this group it is not wise either to criticize Rajneesh and his practices or to use logic and reason to contradict his teaching. At first it is better to ask them questions about their childhood or their life prior to joining the group. Encourage them to talk about their families and experiences that were special to them. Pray for opportunities to share what you believe and then compare the guru's teaching with that of Jesus Christ. When a person leaves a community like this he or she will need much love and support.

Discussion starters

1. Why were these groups initially attractive in the 1960s and 1970s?

2. Share any experience you or your family or friends have had of these groups. If you have met these groups on the streets, seen them on TV, read about them in the papers or attended any of their lectures, what impression did they make on you?

3. Followers of Krishna emphasize the importance of devotion to Krishna: 'An action is bound to be good if it is done out of love for Krishna; it is bad if it is not' (p 120). How do you respond to this claim?

4. In what other ways does ISKCON differ from Christianity in its beliefs and practices? (See p 121-122).

5. What would there be in your church to attract a young person who was getting interested in the cults because of their idealism and demand for total commitment?

6. The sign over the door of the Pune headquarters of Bhagwan Shree Rajneesh reads, 'Shoes and minds are to be left here at the gate' (p 123). What does the Bible teach about the use of the mind? (See Matthew 22:34-40 and Romans 12:2.)

7. In what ways can Christians encourage meditation? What dangers are there in opening ourselves to the Osho techniques of meditation?

10

Yoga, Transcendental Meditation

YOGA

'Since the late nineteen-fifties, when it experienced an unprecedented boom in popularity, yoga has come to be accepted by the majority of the British public as a safe, ordinary, health-giving physical practice; about as occult as jogging or weightlifting; an acceptable Women's Institute activity, alongside flower-arranging, basket-weaving and poetry reading; and nothing whatsoever to do with religion.' (*Yoga*, John Allen, IVP)

Many church halls are used for yoga classes and some doctors and physiotherapists recommend it for the terminally ill, or for rehabilitation after injury, for stress conditions and for post-natal therapy. Most British people think of yoga as a system for keeping fit – someone sitting cross-legged on a mat doing exercises. But this is only one aspect of yoga.

In Chapter 7 we saw that yoga has its origins in Hindu philosophy and that the word, yoga, means to yoke or to unite. In Hindu philosophy yoga is directed to the stilling of conflicting impulses within a person so that he can find his true Self and then be united with ultimate cosmic reality, Brahman. To achieve this a person needs to be freed from the consequences of his actions which result in his being trapped in a cycle of death and re-birth. He also needs to be freed from the illusion which is this material world.

There are many different forms of yoga. The eight disciplines of *Raja yoga* form the basis of most yoga systems today.

One of these disciplines is physical exercise, but this is designed to bring about mastery of the body so that the body does not distract a person's spiritual concentration. They are not merely to improve a person's health or figure. Another discipline is the mastery of breathing techniques in order to control the vital energy which enters the body through breath. A further two disciplines concern concentration and meditation. The purpose of all eight is to unite the person with Brahman. If a person pursues all the disciplines it is said that he or she will gain paranormal knowledge and powers. Many yogis have become famous for their supernatural abilities. But other exponents of yoga will teach that these powers are only a by-product of the disciplines and should not be sought for their own sake.

The most common form of yoga practised in the West is *Hatha yoga*. *Ha* means 'moon' and *tha*, 'sun'. Yogis believe that there are two currents in the body, one from the sun and one from the moon, which are at war with each other, causing restlessness in mind and body. If they can be made to work together a person can be free to concentrate on his true Self. The three activities of Hatha yoga – the physical exercises, the rules of hygiene and diet and the methods of breath control – are designed to be used together to unite the two currents. This leaves the person free to direct the life-energy that comes into the body through his breath to the spiritual energy centre at the base of the spine. This is said to make the spiritual life easier and it can be used to release supernatural powers. Many in the West only see Hatha yoga as a system of health-giving exercises, whereas many in the East would see it as being the preliminary form of exercise before real yoga begins.

There are many other types of yoga in Hinduism. *Gnana yoga* uses meditation on the Hindu scriptures, wisdom and experience to get in touch with the true Self and gain absolute knowledge.

Karma yoga teaches that work should not be done for personal fulfilment or for the satisfaction of personal gain, but as worship. Mahatma Gandhi, its most famous exponent, said, 'Satisfaction should be sought in the work done, not in its outcome.' The results of a man's actions are God's responsibility.

Bhakti yoga teaches the use of bhakti – devotion – to one of the personal forms of god like Vishnu or Krishna in order to realize the true Self, which is hidden by the illusion of physical reality, and to escape from the cycle of birth and death. Bhakti yoga includes the chanting of mantras as one way of showing devotion. It is this form of yoga which has been popularized by ISKCON. The movement's devotees use it to escape from the illusion of the material world in order to devote themselves to the worship of Krishna, the supreme reality. *The British Wheel of Yoga* teaches mainly Hatha yoga but also encourages 'integral yoga' which includes Hatha, Gnana, Karma, Bhakti and Raja yogas.

It is interesting to note that in his book, *Perfection of Yoga*, Swami Prabhupada of ISKCON says that those who use pseudo forms of yoga which simply involve exercising and deep breathing will not find any spiritual benefit. Other responsible Hindu yogis deplore the excessive use of magical powers or the encouragement of occult or spiritual forces. The true yogi should concentrate on seeking a deeper experience of Brahman and not be diverted into these areas.

Among the many forms of yoga there is also *Tantric yoga*. Most yoga involves discipline and self-denial but tantric encourages the use of the natural impulses of the body to aid the experience of ultimate reality. Sexual relations especially are seen as a means to experience the ultimate oneness of the universe. This is the type of yoga which lay behind the teaching of Bhagwan Shree Rajneesh.

Yoga is found not only in Hinduism but also in Sikhism, Buddhism, Taoism and Jainism. Surprisingly it is also found in Sufism, a sect of Islam. Islam affirms a personal God, as do Judaism and Christianity, and so the adoption of yoga by Sufis indicates that they are departing from the basic beliefs of Islam.

Because of its underlying philosophy and ultimate goal of absorption into Brahman, Christians should not be involved in yoga. If as Christians we wish to do exercises it is better to go to a keep-fit class! Yoga encourages a preoccupation with self, typical of the second half of the twentieth century. It encourages self-knowledge, self-realization, self-development, self-fulfilment, self-satisfaction, and even self-redemption instead of salvation in Christ. The concentration on self and the discipline of 'withdrawal', another of the eight disciplines, can lead to a mental passivity that leaves a person open to occult influence. Exponents of yoga also teach that all religions are true and one is no more valid than another. This, of course, directly contradicts the Christian view of revelation and the uniqueness of Christ. It is a shame that many Christians fail to show the same dedication and self-discipline in Christian living as those who practise yoga show in that discipline. For those who wish to witness to people involved in yoga it will be good if they have experience of biblical meditation, spiritual discipline and sacrifice. If a person has been involved in the magical forms of yoga it may be necessary to pray for their release from spiritual bondage.

TRANSCENDENTAL MEDITATION

In 1959 another Hindu guru left India to spread his teaching in the West. He was Maharishi Mahesh Yogi (*Mahanshi* = Great Sage; *Mahesh* is the family name; *Yogi* = one who has achieved union with God). Unlike the founder of ISKCON he didn't teach devotion to Lord Krishna but he offered 'spiritual growth, peace and happiness through a system of deep meditation'. He claims to have been the favourite follower of Guru Dev in India and that Dev sent him away to devise a new technique which would make his Hindu teaching acceptable internationally.

At first the technique of Transcendental Meditation (known simply as TM) was not popular in India, Britain or America. But in 1967 the Beatles and some other famous personalities showed interest, easily affording the high fees to take the course, and its popularity increased. In 1965 there had only been 220 meditators, but by the end of 1968 there were 12,000.

Maharishi introduced reduced fees for students, set up the Students International Meditation Society and drew in the American youth who were looking for something new. He marketed the system, as he does in Britain, not as a religion but as a natural technique developed in India that provides people with deep rest, improves clarity of perception, develops creative intelligence, expands awareness and ensures full development of the individual.

By 1970 Maharishi had an income of $20 million a year and there were 6,000 trained teachers of Transcendental Meditation. The movement was widely accepted in the States with courses being held in schools, colleges, universities and even in the Army. In 1978 Mentmore Towers in Buckinghamshire was bought for £250,000 as the main British centre. By 1980 some 75,000 British people had been initiated and a thousand more were said to be initiated every month. By 2000 there were 35,000 meditators in Ireland alone and five million worldwide. Classes in Transcendental Meditation are advertised in local papers, in public libraries, in colleges and universities and the technique is even taught in some schools and adopted by some large business companies.

The basic technique of Transcendental Meditation is simple. Each person is given a mantra, a secret sound to repeat and meditate on for twenty minutes morning and evening. Regular meditation is claimed to reduce tension and increase energy. The effects are said to be scientifically verifiable and the technique is described as 'the practical aspects of the Science of Creative Intelligence'. In the stress of modern society this has a wide appeal to many students, business and professional people.

Maharishi has opened centres and universities in many countries to spread Transcendental Meditation and the Natural Law teaching found in Vedic literature throughout the world. He planned to set up 3,600 centres, each to train 1000 teachers, to pass on the technique to the 100,000,000 people in its area. At the time of the Gulf War he was convinced that if one person in every hundred practised the technique of TM crime would decrease and war would cease. In 1991 he founded the World Center of Perfect Health and World Peace in Iowa. Besides offering healthcare and enlightenment it was established 'to raise the number of Yogic Flyers to 7,000, thus ensuring an integrated national consciousness and peace in the world, – a fertile ground for Heaven on Earth'. Since 1997 he has been celebrating the onset of Global Administration through Natural Law supporting National law – the way to bring peace and heaven on earth.

After forty years he still has great vision. His personal and world goals seem admirable and the simplicity of the technique sounds like an easy solution to reaching Utopia both personally and globally. 'Health, Happiness and Long Life – public lectures on this scientifically validated programme', read the advertisement for Transcendental Meditation in the local paper. At British universities and colleges an invitation was given to students to attend an introductory talk: 'Enlightenment – the TM programme – to create an ideal society'. At the time of the General Election we were invited to vote for the Natural Law Party 'to create a government with the ability to satisfy everyone'.

Psychiatrists have said it would be equally helpful for a person's health if they lay on a couch and read a book for twenty minutes morning and evening. Relaxing for forty minutes a day is good for our physical health. Meditation is encouraged in the Bible, but it is meditation on God (Psalm 63:6), on his works (Psalms 77:12; 143:5) and on his law (Psalm 119:15). In Transcendental Meditation the initiate is encouraged to open his mind, not to concentrate on anything but 'to allow it to submerge into a deeper level of consciousness'. Opening the mind in this way has different effects on different people. Some relax, others become anxious, confused, frustrated, withdrawn or depressed and a few believe that it has allowed them to become possessed by a spirit. After giving up Transcendental Meditation some find it difficult to concentrate their minds on serious study, to relate closely to others or to shake off spiritual oppression. Transcendental Meditation claims it is a harmless technique to help people to relax and be at peace with themselves, but it seems that many find it has dangerous side effects, so its benefits are difficult 'to verify scientifically'.

Its religious nature

Transcendental Meditation claims that it is not religious, but is a technique that will help a person become a better follower of his or her own religion. This claim has been successfully challenged in the American courts (with the result that it is no longer taught in state schools), and in the Danish courts. At the initiation ceremony the words spoken by the teacher are in Sanskrit so the initiate does not usually understand what is said. They include, however, a prayer of adoration to many Hindu gods, including Brahman, Vishnu and Shiva and even to Guru Dev, the Maharashi's original teacher. Guru Dev is spoken of as 'the Eternal, the Pure, Immovable . . . the embodiment of pure knowledge which is beyond and above the universe like the sky', an incarnation of the divine. The mantras are closely linked with the names of Hindu gods. This implicit acknowledgement of the deity of other gods is, of course, incompatible with the monotheism of Christianity, Judaism and Islam.

Initiates are encouraged to aspire to higher levels of consciousness. Maharishi teaches that people normally live on the first three levels of consciousness: sleeping, dreaming, waking; but through meditation the initiate can aspire to transcendental consciousness and cosmic consciousness. The fourth level of consciousness, transcendental consciousness, is achieved when the body is free from its five senses; it is in a state of physical rest but the mind is awake. The person is in a state of 'restful wakefulness'. The fifth level, cosmic consciousness, is achieved when a follower can hold the transcendental state permanently and so be at peace without stress.

Those who follow Transcendental Meditation for many years may go on to the highest levels of consciousness: level six, God consciousness; level seven, unity consciousness and Brahman consciousness. Hindu philosophy clearly underlies these concepts.

The ideal of monistic Hinduism is that the individual self (atman) should be absorbed into, or become at one with, ultimate reality (Brahman). Christianity teaches that Christ has made us one with God in the sense of being able to have a personal relationship with him, the barrier of our sins being removed. This type of Hinduism and Transcendental Meditation teaches that the ultimate goal is for the individual to no longer exist but become absorbed into God. Technically, it is not a *process* but a *perception*.

Christian witness

As Christians it is difficult to witness to people involved in Transcendental Meditation. Usually the meditators will feel superior to you and not wish to learn from you. If they have been badly affected by their attempts to meditate they may not be able to follow logical reasoning; they will in any case have been warned against confusing themselves with other religious views. Try to find out what it was that led them to learn the technique, and pray for opportunities to speak of how Christ can satisfy the desires they felt then. If they are nominal Christians you may be able to discuss with them the possible dangers of the system they are following and its implicit association with Hinduism. Encourage them to explore instead the long tradition of Christian meditation which follows the example of the psalmist in thoughtful meditation on God, his works and his law.

If a person wishes to give up Transcendental Meditation to investigate Christianity you will need to reassure him of his value as an individual both to God and to man, and make clear the biblical distinction between God and his creation. You will need to explain the work of Christ in reconciling God and man. There may also be a need for prayer for healing of the mind and for deliverance from spiritual oppression or even possession.

Discussion starters

1. Share any experiences you or your friends or family have had of either yoga or TM.

2. What is the ultimate goal of yoga? In the light of the underlying Hindu philosophy, do you think it is advisable for Christians to practise yoga? Why or why not?

3. What would you say to a young Christian who asked your advice about doing yoga exercises?

4. Why do you think TM has become very popular in the West? What is its attraction? What are its dangers?

5. Maharishi Mahesh Yogi offered 'spiritual growth, peace and happiness through a system of deep meditation' (p 129). Is there anything wrong with this? How does Transcendental Meditation differ from Christian meditation in its aims, method and subject matter?

6. What would you say to a friend who was using the technique of TM or beginning to show an interest in it?

7. What is the value of Christian meditation? Is it something you should spend more time exploring and if so, how will you go about it?

PART III

New Western Religious Movements

Introduction

In Part Two we have looked at some of the new religious movements that have their origin in Hinduism. In Part Three we will consider some of the religious movements of the nineteenth and twentieth centuries which have deviated from orthodox Christianity. Unfortunately there have been so many that we cannot consider them all.

We will look first at five groups which began in the nineteenth century (Jehovah's Witnesses, The Mormons, Christadelphians, Christian Scientists and Seventh-Day Adventists). The first two of these are still proselytizing and growing. Then we will look at two that began in the second half of this century (The Unification Church and The Family of Love). We can compare how they deviated from orthodoxy originally and whether there are any lessons or warnings for us today. Other questions to consider are how far their deviations are spiritual, moral or doctrinal.

We have not dealt in detail with Spiritualists, another group which emerged during this period. In animist religions and in many Eastern religions contact with the spirit world is encouraged. In the Old and New Testament sections of the Bible the existence of spirits and the ability to communicate with them is not denied, but the practice of getting in touch with them is expressly forbidden. It is a subject of debate how far Joseph Smith, the founder of Mormonism, was influenced by spiritism, but there is no question that founders of groups since have been strongly influenced. The Unification Church and the Family were both founded by Christians who were subject to spirit visitations. We will also be able to trace the influence of Eastern religious ideas in the second half of the nineteenth century and then in the twentieth century. Mary

Baker Eddy of Christian Science adapted Christianity to fit an Eastern view of God and the world. In the 1960s Moon followed suit. So although we do not go into detail about Spiritualism it has influenced many of the groups we shall consider.

In some of the groups there have been deviations from the moral teaching of Christianity. The Mormons originally encouraged polygamy although it was not the common practice of nineteenth-century America. In the twentieth century the Moonies encouraged the telling of lies when it is for the good of the church – 'Heavenly deception'. The Children of God, now known as The Family, have encouraged their girls to seduce men in order to show them how much God loves them. Until the scare of AIDS they also encouraged 'free love' among their members to spread the love of God.

But as we look at the groups in more detail we shall see that the biggest area of deviation is doctrinal.

Where do they find their source of authority? Many groups will claim to be based on the Bible, but so often it is their founder's interpretation of the Bible and their founder's own writings which become their chief source of authority.

The divinity of Christ is usually disputed by these groups. Jesus was merely a man created by God like other men and used by him for a special task but he is not divine. The Holy Spirit too is only thought of as the power of God, except by the Family who consider him to be a female spirit! Some also have unorthodox views about God the Father. He is not distinct from man; man can attain divinity. This means that most of these groups deny the doctrine of the Trinity. Even if at first sight they seem to believe in God the Father, his son Jesus Christ and the Holy Spirit, it is important to ascertain what they mean by these titles. Before we criticize or accept a new group we need to understand what they mean by the terms they use.

The other area in which these groups deviate from Christian orthodoxy is salvation. 'By grace you have been saved, through faith - and this not from yourselves, it is the gift of God - not by works, so that no-one can boast'

(Ephesians 2:8-9). The Christian church teaches that Christ died for our sins to bring us back to God and we serve and obey him out of gratitude for his love. But the sects and cults teach that we need to earn our salvation by our own efforts, keeping all the commandments, or visiting, or using time and energy for the leader or the movement, or by putting our thinking right (Christian Science emphasizes the last point). All these different ways by which we may earn salvation contradict the Bible's teaching on grace.

Why do people join these movements?

Some people automatically assume that those who join religious movements like those in Parts Two and Three do so because they are rebelling against their parents or because they have an inadequate relationship with them. Either of these reasons may be true, but there are many other possibilities. There are probably as many reasons as there are members!

Most of the people who join are idealistic and have a sincere desire to help others. Some are naive or curious and get swept along by persuasive members of the groups. Some are seeking a sense of identity and worth which they find within the clear parameters of one of these groups. Others are genuinely seeking a religion or religious experience. Many appreciate the authoritative teaching and strong leadership. Some say they tried a Christian church and found there was no teaching, or no love among the members, or no concern for those outside. Others were church members but saw in these groups greater commitment to their teaching and their organization. It has been said that the sects are 'the unpaid debts of the church'.

In groups such as The People's Temple in the USA, 'born-again' Christians found a church which initially showed love and concern for its members, a close fellowship, social concern and a total commitment to the lordship of Jesus. But the leader then abused his position of authority by making total demands on the members' time and money and exercising discipline which would not have disgraced a totalitarian state.

This led to the tragic massacre in Jonestown, Guyana in 1978. That affected cult recruitment for some years. However, by the 1990s intelligent, idealistic individuals were again willing to commit themselves to new cults, sects and religious movements. Some of these groups, based in Canada, the USA, Switzerland and Japan, have committed group suicides or caused the deaths of others.

Once people realize that their trust and commitment have been abused it is difficult for them to leave such a movement because it has become their family, and their friends are within it. Many of those who have joined a cult will have given over their money and property to it and, even if the leaders do not make them afraid to leave, they fear the outside world. The more deeply people are involved in these groups the harder it will be for them to leave.

A particular problem which faces those who leave the cults is their gradual realization of what they have allowed others to do to them. This makes it very difficult for them to re-establish a genuine self-respect and sense of worth. They desperately need to know that God loves them totally, just as they are, and they need gentle, continuous help to begin to take responsibility for their own lives.

11

Jehovah's Witnesses

Almost everyone in Britain has heard of Jehovah's Witnesses, 'those people who are always knocking on our doors!'

Today their approach is much more polite and less pushing than it used to be. As one senior Jehovah's Witness explained, 'We have realized there are enough people interested in what we are saying that we have no need to force our teaching on the unwilling.' When you open the door some will openly tell you that they are Jehovah's Witnesses doing their visiting.

If you live in a town or city near one of their meeting places you will be visited every two or three months. Usually two people will come, a trainer and a trainee. Their opening remarks are often about the state of the world today and the need for hope. Some will ask if you have any religious views and their further comments will vary according to whether you do or not. If you say you are a church member, they may talk about an issue like church unity. After talking with you for a while they will offer to sell you one of their magazines. If you buy one they will come back in a month to see if you are interested in discussing their teaching. One person may then visit you regularly and encourage you to have a group in your house to study the Bible. If you agree you will actually study one of their publications with Bible verses printed in it – not the Bible itself. The next step will be to invite you to join a small group of Jehovah's Witnesses meeting in one of their houses. Later you will be invited to their local meeting place, the Kingdom Hall. There you will have lectures and teaching sessions based on the *Watchtower* magazine, before you in turn are asked to go out visiting door-to-door. After this, the final stage in becoming a Jehovah's Witness is baptism. Former members of the group feel it is very hard for a person to leave after they have been baptized.

Origins

In 1852 Charles Russell was born into a Presbyterian family in the USA. As a young teenager working in his father's shop he used to write texts on the wall in the hope of converting passing workmen. Then, after a few years as an agnostic, he began studying the Bible again through the influence of an Adventist movement (see chapter 13). He concluded that the churches were wrong in much of their doctrine, chiefly with regard to the trinity, the deity of Christ and hell. So at the age of eighteen Russell gathered a group of people around him to study the Bible. Four years later he sold his father's shop and devoted himself to Bible studies, preaching and teaching.

Influenced by the Adventist teaching of the mid-nineteenth century he made his first forecast about Christ's second coming. Christ had come invisibly, he said, and in three and a half years he would set up his kingdom. When this prophecy was shown to be inaccurate many were left disappointed and disillusioned, but he still had thirty disciples in his congregation at Pittsburg. Within a year of the publication of the first edition of the *Watch Tower* magazine there were thirty congregations in Pennsylvania and the neighbouring states. These people were known as 'Russellites' and were a loose association of his followers.

Zion's Watch Tower Tract Society was established in 1884. At the head of the organization was the President, Charles Russell, with six other directors. The name was later changed to Watch Tower Bible and Tract Society.

At this time Russell published his book, *Studies in the Scriptures*, setting out his own views. His followers claimed that these volumes were indispensable to understanding the Bible.

Around the turn of the century Russell visited England four times and set up an office in London. By 1914 England had 1,200 congregations, 15,000 active followers of his teaching and 55,000 subscribers to the *Watchtower* magazine.

This was despite disappointment over another prophecy of Christ's return. Russell had taught that Christ returned invisibly in 1874 and would set up his kingdom in 1914. When his prediction failed to come true, the Witnesses said that 1914 'marked the end of the Gentile times'. Russell died in 1916.

Judge Rutherford succeeded him as President, having previously been Russell's legal adviser. Rutherford was a good speaker and a strong, authoritarian leader who gathered up the loose association of democratic congregations and set up a unified, bureaucratic organization. He claimed to desire 'divine control, not human control'. Elders were no longer appointed by local congregations, but a hierarchical system was enforced with the society appointing all the leaders. The *Watchtower* magazine was to be studied in groups to ensure doctrinal uniformity.

In 1918 he was imprisoned for anti-war talk but was released the following year a 'hero' and a 'martyr'. Again he predicted the end of the world, this time in 1925.

'Jehovah's Witnesses' was the name adopted by the group in 1931. When Rutherford died in 1942 he was succeeded by his vice-president, Nathan Knorr. Knorr proved to be a very good organizer and under his direction there was great growth in the worldwide organization. But in 1975 members were lost again by another failed prediction about the second coming. F.W. Franz became leader on Knorr's death in 1977.

Organization and practice

The Jehovah's Witnesses headquarters are in Brooklyn, New York. The organization is still controlled by a triumvirate of the President, his vice-president, and the secretary/treasurer, and with the involvement of four other directors. They have divided the whole world into zones, branches, districts, circuits and congregations for the purposes of evangelism and administration.

It is not possible to be a member of the Jehovah's Witnesses until you are doing ten hours door-to-door visiting per month and selling at least twelve magazines. 'Pioneers' have to do 100 hours a month and special pioneers 140 hours. Many keen members take part-time jobs in order to give themselves time to visit more frequently. Some are retired people or housewives.

They do not call themselves a church – 'Churches are of the devil' – and they do not have worship services. Their centres are the Kingdom Halls where they meet for teaching, study, training and planning. Their teaching and study is based on the subject of the latest *Watchtower* magazine which is published every two weeks in 131 languages. Over 22 million were sold each fortnight in 2000.

Mass baptisms and assemblies are held – in Britain they have been held at places like Twickenham Rugby Ground and the former Wembley stadium. A memorial service is held once a year on the night of Jesus' death, Passover night. All Jehovah's Witnesses are expected to attend, but only a few special members, who believe they are of the 144,000 mentioned in Revelation, are allowed to take the bread and wine.

The Witnesses are well known for not celebrating Christmas, Easter or birthdays and they will not allow their children to study RE in school. Blood transfusions are also forbidden.

They never serve in their country's army, vote or give allegiance to any earthly state, so they always suffer under totalitarian regimes. They suffered under Hitler in Germany and until recently in what was the Soviet Union. In the 1980s many were martyred in Mozambique and many others became refugees. They are not permitted in Singapore.

By 1980 there were more than two million Jehovah's Witnesses in over 200 countries, and six million people attended their memorial services worldwide. In Britain there were 77,000 Witnesses. With the opening up of Eastern Europe in 1990 the number of Witnesses in the world increased quickly

to three and a half million. By 2000 they had six million practising members in 235 countries and over fourteen million
attended their memorial services worldwide. There were over
126,000 in Britain. Their greatest increase in numbers is now in
the non-Western world.

Beliefs

Some of the Witnesses' beliefs are similar to those of orthodox
Christianity. But as with many of the sects which are deviations from Christianity, they conflict with orthodox Christian
beliefs on the issues of authority, the deity of Christ and the
way of salvation. We will consider six of the most significant
areas of doctrine.

Authority

Witnesses claim that the Bible is God's word, that it is truth
and that they gain all their beliefs from it. But the Bible must
always be studied through the *Watchtower* publications, so the
Society, rather than the Bible, becomes their authority. They
prefer to use their own (highly interpretative) New World
Translation of the Bible. The *Watchtower* interpretations of
individual verses are learnt without question and without reference to the context. So, for example, Leviticus 17:14, Genesis
9:3-4 and Acts 15:28-29 are said to prohibit blood transfusions.

God

They call God 'Jehovah' which is an attempt to transliterate
the Hebrew name YHWH. They call themselves his witnesses
because of the statement in Isaiah 43:10, ' "You are my witnesses" declares the Lord.' He is the only one to whom we
should offer praise and worship. All other beings have been
created by him, including his son, Jesus Christ. Witnesses
agree with Jewish scholars that God is One and deny any
sense of plurality within the Godhead. As with Judaism,

Witnesses draw this teaching from Deuteronomy 6:4, 'Hear O Israel: the Lord our God, the Lord is one.'However, the word 'one' which is used here is the same as that used of a married couple in Genesis 2:24, 'they will become one flesh', so it is not necessary to reject the concept of the Trinity on these grounds.

Jesus Christ

Witnesses teach that Jesus is a son of God, inferior to Jehovah. Before his birth he was a spirit, the Archangel Michael, the first of God's creation. On earth he was a man who died on a stake not a cross, and was raised from the dead, once more as an immortal spirit. There was no physical resurrection and what happened to the body is unimportant. This contrasts with the New Testament writers' teaching on the nature of Jesus in John 1:1-5, Colossians 1:15-20 and Hebrews 1:1-4, and these are some of the passages they interpret differently from orthodox Christianity. Their teaching also contradicts Jesus' view of himself as represented in John's Gospel, especially in the 'I am', sayings, his claim to have authority to forgive sins, and his acceptance of Thomas's words, 'My Lord and my God'. The difficulty of their view is highlighted by a statement of C.S. Lewis: 'Jesus, the Jew, must have been a fraud or a charlatan, a megalomaniac, or indeed God.'

Salvation

Witnesses believe that Satan gained control of the earth because of Adam's sin. Jehovah sent Michael to earth as the perfect man, Jesus, to die to pay a ransom to Satan. This removed the death penalty for those human beings who can then merit eternal life by denial of the world and devotion to Jehovah and his organization. So Christ's death only makes salvation possible for the few, and the few have to earn it. It is not a free gift of God.

The Holy Spirit

One of their books, *Let God be True*, states that the 'Holy Spirit is the invisible active force of Almighty God that moves his servants to do his will'. There is no belief in the Holy Spirit as a person or as divine. He is regarded only as a force. Witnesses do not know that the Holy Spirit can be in them, giving them God's power and presence and developing in them the fruits of the Spirit such as love, joy and peace. Theirs is a religion of duty.

The Kingdom

This is often the main concern of their teaching. They believe Christ returned invisibly in 1914 and so we are now in the end time. The present world systems are evil and will end at the battle of Har-Mageddon. The wicked will be eternally destroyed and the 144,000, the anointed who have been most obedient, will rule in heaven. The other faithful members of the Witnesses will reign on earth with Christ for one thousand years and will be joined by those who died without a chance to hear the truth. At the end of the thousand years those who have rejected Jehovah will be annihilated and the others will live for ever on the renewed Eden-like earth in Christ's kingdom.

Christian witness

As our friendships with Jehovah's Witnesses develop it is helpful to know why they became Witnesses. Some are born into a Witness family so are brought up to follow their parents' example in practice and belief. Others are seeking God or a religious experience and are either visited by a Witness, or may have tried their local church and been disappointed by its lack of teaching or pastoral care. Yet others are looking for answers to the world's problems. Some are lonely or bereaved and, in the first place, they enjoy a visit by someone who will listen to them. Then they appreciate the sense of belonging to a home group and later to an organization.

Jehovah's Witnesses who have become Christians say that the things they appreciate about their new faith are: freedom to serve God, rather than bondage to rules; assurance of eternal life now rather than always striving for some distant hope in the future; a personal relationship with a God you can know and who cares for you; and a new enjoyment in prayer and worship.

So it is good to talk with them about God's grace, his forgiveness, his love and mercy. Witnesses have no certainty of eternal life with God because such a 'reward' depends to a large extent, in their eyes, on their own work and effort. Some may value being guided to passages such as Romans 5:6-11 and 8:1-17 where Paul writes of our absolute assurance of salvation because of the work Christ has done.

Witnesses are also taught that our churches are dead and that no young people go. If we can introduce them to groups of lively, witnessing, believing young Christians it can cast doubt on the teaching they have received.

We can also tell them that God can speak to us directly through the Bible; he is not restricted to speaking through the *Watchtower* magazine. With some Witnesses it may be right to point out the false prophecies of the past and the *Watchtower*'s misinterpretation of Scripture.

If you are hospitable to Witnesses you may be able to testify in practical ways to what Jesus means to you, as well as showing them truths from the Bible that they have not learned in their set texts. An ex-Witness who is now a Baptist pastor said it was the love of Christians and their willingness to spend time talking with him and his wife in their homes that caused them to leave the Witnesses. Another man left after twenty-three years because his father kept sending him literature which explained where the *Watchtower*'s teachings were wrong. Eventually the son was sufficiently provoked to do some serious study and came to the conclusion that his father was right!

Discussion starters

1. How often have you been visited by Jehovah's Witnesses? How did they open the conversation? Share any other experience you have had of contact with Witnesses.

2. Do you think it is a good idea for all Christians to engage Witnesses in conversation or to invite them to their homes? Give your reasons.

3. What do you believe about the person of Jesus Christ? Where do you find that teaching in the Bible? Study one of the passages about the person of Jesus listed on p 146, then divide into pairs. One of you should try to explain the passage to the other, while the other is free to respond with the arguments of a Jehovah's Witness. Change roles after a few minutes.

   Together, discuss the problems you encountered and possible ways of overcoming them.

4. How would you explain to a Jehovah's Witness how they may be saved and gain eternal life?

5. Read the verses which Witnesses use to oppose blood transfusions (see p 145). What do these verses mean in their context?

6. How would you interpret passages like 2 Peter 3:7-13 and Revelation 21:1-2 to a Witness looking forward to living on this earth for ever?

7. An experience which Jehovah's Witnesses do not have is that of a personal relationship with Jesus Christ. How would you go about sharing with a Witness what Jesus means to you?

12

The Church of Jesus Christ of the Latter-Day Saints

Members of this church, who are known as Mormons, are well known in Britain today. Many people have been visited by them. Often the visitors will be two young men, smartly dressed in suits, perhaps wearing hats and usually with American accents. The records of the well-trained Mormon Temple choir have made them familiar to many, while others remember the Osmond family singers, popular in the seventies. In the early part of the twentieth century they were well known because of their practice of polygamy. But since the war they have stressed the importance of the family, have become involved in social work and have acquired a more respectable image.

There are eleven million Mormons in the world, of whom half live in the USA and over a million in Canada, Central and South America. Others are in Europe, South Africa, Australia, New Zealand and East Asia. Until 1978 there were few in black Africa because, until then, no black man was allowed to become a Mormon priest. Now their numbers are increasing rapidly in West Africa. In Britain there were over 150,000 Mormons in 1990 and the numbers there and worldwide seem to be doubling every fifteen years. Their materials are produced in eighty-five languages, but translators are now working to expand the number of languages to more than 200. Strong factors in this growth have been their new image since the war, their adoption of modern sales techniques and the sacrificial devotion of each family in financing their young people as missionaries for two years. In 2000 there were over 60,000 of these young missionaries throughout the world.

Their beliefs originated with Joseph Smith but they have since been altered and elaborated by other leaders of the church. They use the Bible, but they believe it has been superceded by the revelations and teaching of their founder, as well as by their subsequent presidents.

Origins

The Church's founder, Joseph Smith, was born in Vermont, USA, in 1805. During his childhood his parents moved to New York state. At this time the state was going through a time of religious ferment and economic difficulty. The Baptist Church there divided into five denominations and the Methodists into four splinter groups. Many communes and revivalist groups emerged, including the Shakers and the followers of Jemima Wilkinson, who claimed to be a female Christ.

Many people were fascinated by the question of where the 'original' American came from. One popular answer was that they were the lost tribe of Israel. So Joseph Smith and others used to spend time digging up ancient burial mounds, looking for evidence and hidden treasure, a common enough activity in the poverty of those times.

When his family first moved to New York state they had understandable problems in deciding which of the profusion of churches to join. Most of his family joined the Presbyterian Church but he was confused by their conflicting claims. Following the Bible's advice, 'If any of you lacks wisdom, he should ask God' (James 1:5), he went to some woods nearby to pray for guidance. There, he said, two persons appeared to him. One pointed to the other and said, 'This is my beloved son. Hear him.' When he asked what church he should join, he was forbidden to join any because 'all their creeds are an abomination'. Joseph Smith was fourteen at this time.

In 1823 when he was almost eighteen he had a second vision. A magnificent visitor in white, called Moroni, came and told him God had a special task for him. Moroni told him of a book, written by the prophet Mormon on gold plates and buried with two stones, Urim and Thummim, needed for translation. The book contained the story of the previous inhabitants of North America and also the true gospel which had been given to them personally by Jesus. Smith was not allowed by Moroni to dig the plates up then, but he visited the place where they were buried, on the hill Cumorah near Palmyra, once a year for four years.

When he was twenty-one he was allowed to remove the plates for translation. The uneducated Smith sat on one side of a room, behind a blanket, translating the book of Mormon from Reformed Egyptian. Martin Harris, a farmer, sat on the other side writing down the translation. This took a total of three years and then the plates were given back to Moroni. Harris also financed the publication but his wife did not approve. Harris and others claimed to have seen the golden plates, but years later some denied their original testimony. Others again claimed to have seen them with 'the eye of faith'.

The Book of Mormon

The Book of Mormon addressed the problem of who used to live in ancient America and revealed that the main characters in its history were two Jewish brothers, Nephi and Laman. With the rest of their family they emigrated to America from Jerusalem in about 600 BC. Laman disobeyed God and regularly harrassed Nephi, who was pious and obedient. So God cursed Laman and his family and they became dark skinned. These two groups, the Lamanites and the Nephites, spread all across North and South America. Because of their faithful obedience to God the Nephites were rewarded with a visit from the resurrected Jesus Christ, who preached the original gospel to them. Later they were all destroyed by the Lamanites, but not before one Nephite, Mormon, had written down the story. In AD 421 his son, Moroni (who later appeared to Joseph Smith) buried it near Palmyra. The North American Indians are the surviving descendants of the Lamanites.

There are severe problems with accepting the authenticity of the Book of Mormon. The story reads like fiction rather than fact and there is no answer to why Jews travelling from Jerusalem in 600 BC should use an otherwise unknown language of Reformed Egyptian. Many passages in the Book of Mormon appear to be the same as in the King James Version of the Bible written in AD 1611 and yet the Book of Mormon is supposed to have been written about AD 400. There is a preoccupation with the doctrinal problems of the 1820s, such as infant baptism, the Trinity, eternal punishment and even Freemasonry. One passage alleges that Jews brought elephants and pigs to America! It was claimed to be without error, yet 3,000 changes have been made since 1830. To a well-informed Christian the whole book reads like a hoax, but not to an ill-informed, innocent person looking for the truth and a group to which to belong.

The developing church

The year after the publication of the Book of Mormon the 'Church of Jesus Christ of the Latter-Day Saints' was founded. Many Americans found the story preposterous and their claims to be the only true church objectionable, so Mormons were bitterly opposed and hounded from place to place. Their unpopularity was increased by their practice of polygamy – Joseph Smith had forty-eight wives – and the failure of many of their business ventures. In 1844 a group of Mormons attacked the office of a newspaper which had opposed them. Smith and others were subsequently jailed, but a mob stormed the jail and killed him. Immediately Joseph Smith became a martyr to the Mormons.

After his murder there were splits in the church over who should succeed him and many of these breakaway groups still exist today in the States. Brigham Young became President of the main group. Having been driven from one state to another, in 1846 they were expelled by Illinois and set off west to the Rockies. The account of 'The Great Trek' is an amazing story of survival against the odds, of illness such as cholera, of natural hazards and persecution.

In 1847 they founded Salt Lake City in Utah, which is still the headquarters of the Mormon church. When Young died in 1877 there were 140,000 Mormons. He left £400,000 – a sizeable sum in those days – seventeen wives and fifty-six children. The church continued to teach that polygamy was a good thing because it resulted in the creation of more bodies into which pre-existent souls could be born. But in 1890 polygamy was forbidden because of pressure from the American government and is only found today among small off-shoots of the Mormon church.

The Church today

In the Church of Jesus Christ of the Latter-Day Saints it is still common to have large families, though only one wife. Each child is baptized at the age of eight because it is considered that before then they have no mature understanding of right and wrong. Boys of twelve are ordained in the 'Aaronic priesthood' as a deacon and at sixteen as a priest. At nineteen they are made members of the 'Melchizedek priesthood' and become elders, able to do missionary service. Missionaries are sent out in groups of seventy supervised by the twelve Apostles from Utah. These twelve are under the authority of the President and prophet, who in 2000 was Gordon B. Hinckley. The church claims that these offices of prophet and apostle and the two orders of priesthood died out in New Testament times but were restored by divine revelation to Joseph Smith. Therefore only their church with these restored offices is the true and authoritative church.

Each local area has its own presiding bishop. In Britain their churches tend to be in new towns or on new estates and there is only one temple, which was built in Surrey in 1958. In the States there are many Mormon temples and they have established their own educational system which takes children up to university level. They do not smoke, drink alcohol, coffee or tea, and they disapprove of cola drinks. Meat is only eaten sparingly. Tithing is encouraged so the church flourishes financially, missionary outreach is well supported and provision is made for any members in need.

Beliefs

Authority

In their thirteen articles of faith Mormons say they 'believe the Bible to be the word of God as far as it is translated correctly', and that they believe 'the *Book of Mormon* to be the word of God'. So along with Smith's other works, *Doctrine and Covenants* and *Pearl of Great Price*, the *Book of Mormon* supercedes the Bible. New revelations by their President are also accepted, whether or not they agree with the teaching of the Bible.

The Trinity

'We believe in God, the Eternal Father, and in His Son, Jesus Christ, and in the Holy Ghost.'This teaching on the Trinity sounds orthodox until you discover exactly what Mormons believe about the three persons. Mormons believe God has a body of flesh and bone and that he was once a man, who was later exalted as the god, Elohim. 'As man is now, God once was; as God is now, man may become.' He is one of many gods, the one who created our spirits long ago, and now places our spirits in bodies on earth.

Jesus Christ was the first spirit-child created by God, known as Jehovah in his pre-earth life. Christ was one in purpose with God and sinless, but not God incarnate. He was born to this earth by physical union between Elohim and Mary and was married to the sisters Mary and Martha, and to Mary Magdalene.

It is thought that the Holy Ghost is given only to those who are baptized as Mormons and have received the laying-on of hands by Mormon priests. The Holy Ghost is different from the spirit of God who enlightens all men coming into the world with the knowledge of good and evil.

Mankind

Mormon teaching states that each person has been pre-existent in a spirit world, though on earth we have no memory of that time. We are all Christ's brothers. There has been no fall, because Adam's sin was necessary and good in order that we might know the difference between good and evil. We all have the potential to become gods.

The second coming

Mormons believe in 'the literal gathering of Israel and in the restoration of the Ten Tribes; that Zion (the new Jerusalem) will be upon the American continent; that Christ will reign personally upon the earth; and that the earth will be renewed and receive its paradisiacal glory.' (*Articles of Faith*, number 10.)

Salvation and exaltation

Christ died to save all people from physical death. All will be resurrected, they say, but not all will be exalted to heaven. At the final judgment some may be banished to the realms of Satan. Those who are judged worthy of immortality, but not much else, will enter the lowest heaven, telestial glory. Devout Christians and less devout Mormons will enter terrestrial glory, but devout Mormons will be exalted to the highest heaven, celestial glory. So salvation is of little consequence; Mormons need to earn exaltation. This is gained by faith in their Mormon gospel, by Mormon baptism, church membership and keeping the commandments. Because baptism is so important a Mormon can be baptized on behalf of a dead ancestor. Higher exaltation can be achieved by the laying-on of hands for the priesthood, by temple work and by celestial marriage.

Celestial marriage is permitted for very devout Mormons and involves being married in a Mormon temple. It is believed that such marriages will last for eternity, and that they will be able to have celestial children.

Christian witness

A well-taught Christian who is a member of a lively fellowship is unlikely to be attracted to Mormonism, but it can look very attractive to a young, untaught Christian, to a nominal Christian from a sleepy church or to a seeker after religious truth. The missionaries who come to the door are pleasant young men, convinced of the truth of their gospel and well trained in communication. Mormons are hard working and prosperous, their churches are friendly, lively and caring and they offer plenty of activity to fill your life.

You may find yourself in the position of needing to counsel a young or nominal Christian who is thinking of joining their church. It is important that you don't just attack Mormons over their founder's behaviour, their history or their beliefs. It is better to begin by exploring clearly basic Christian teaching, pointing out where it differs from Mormon beliefs.

When Mormon missionaries come to your door, if you have time and a good knowledge of the Bible invite them in and offer them a drink of milk or fruit juice. They may not be as well drilled in their doctrines as Jehovah's Witnesses are, so are likely to be more open to a well-reasoned account of ortho-dox Christian belief. Ask how they became members of the group, but try to keep the initiative in conversation.

They will be trained to give their testimony, especially about the importance of reading the Book of Mormon to find the truth. Have your Bible to hand and ask them what they believe about God or Jesus, then share what the Bible says. You will need to be familiar with the Book of Mormon in order to be able to draw their attention to places where God's 'revelations' there – about himself, sin, salvation and lifestyle – contradict what he says in the Bible. Both 'revelations' can only be true if God contradicts himself.

If you are a neighbour or colleague of a Mormon it should be possible to form a long-term friendship in which you can discuss your beliefs in more detail. Don't be argumentative, pushing your own views. Rather, ask why they believe a certain point of doctrine and why their teaching disagrees with the Bible.

It is vital to pray for anyone to whom you may be witnessing in this way. The devil is in the business of veiling the truth and keeping people from seeing the light of the gospel and the glory of Christ (2 Corinthians 4:3-1). It is only the Holy Spirit who can open their eyes to see what is true and what is false, and he will guide us in what we say to them and how we approach them.

Discussion starters

1. A member of your youth fellowship is attracted by the Mormon church. Why and how would you try to dissuade him or her from attending or joining the group?

2. Share any experiences you have of meeting Mormons. Where did you meet them? If they witnessed to you how did they do it? How were you able to respond?

3. Explain the orthodox Christian belief about God. What passages of scripture would you use? How would you contrast it with the Mormon view?

4. Contrast the Mormon and Christian teaching about Jesus Christ.

5. How does your view of mankind differ from the Mormon teaching?

6. What does the Bible teach about eternal life? (See John's Gospel.) How do we gain it? When does it begin? How does it differ from the Mormon view of salvation and exaltation?

7. The Mormons place a high value on family life, setting aside one evening a week to be together as a family. They also encourage their young people to play an active and responsible part in church life. What can the Christian church learn from their insights here? In particular, what could your church do to encourage its families and young people?

13

Christadelphianism, Christian Science, Seventh-Day Adventism

The Jehovah's Witnesses and the Mormons are groups that began in the 1800s and are still large and growing today. We will now look more briefly at some other groups that also began in the 1800s and are still found in Britain today, but are not so large or well known. Because the Witnesses and the Mormons do street visiting in the areas near their meeting places most of us have been contacted by them. With groups like the Christadelphians, the Christian Scientists and the Seventh-Day Adventists we may have seen their meeting places but unless we have a relative, a neighbour or a friend who belongs to them we will probably know little about them.

CHRISTADELPHIANISM

There are 330 groups of Christadelphians in Britain but fewer than that in the rest of the world. Most of them are in English-speaking countries. Their name means 'brother of Christ' and their groups are called 'ecclesias'. They arrange well-presented Bible exhibitions and public lectures and offer tracts at large events. In the local paper home Bible studies are advertised and telephone numbers are given where a Bible message can be heard.

In their meeting rooms they have a weekly breaking-of-bread ceremony, a public lecture, a weekly Bible class and a women's meeting. They have no professional clergy or ministers so the meetings are run by lay elders and sometimes they will have visiting speakers from neighbouring assemblies. Most of the women will wear hats, the meetings will be led by men and the Bible will be studied seriously so it may resemble a gathering of the Christian Brethren. One of their websites bemoans the fact that they are in decline and some of their members are becoming evangelical Protestants.

History

The group was founded by Dr John Thomas, an Englishman who sailed to the States in 1832. When he was shipwrecked on the way he vowed that if he was saved he would devote his life to religion. So on arrival in America he studied the Bible deeply and was especially fascinated by the prophets and Revelation. Within two years he had rejected orthodox interpretations and formulated his own views. Convinced his ideas were right he began to publish a magazine to spread his teaching.

In 1848 Thomas came to England and preached throughout the country for two years and wrote a book, *Elpis Israel*, about the Kingdom of God. When he came again in 1862 he found groups which became known as 'Thomasites' in many parts of the country. The largest number were in Birmingham, which still remains the centre of the organization today. Thomas wrote a 2000-page commentary on Revelation called *Eureka*, claiming that he had found the meaning of the book that had baffled scholars for years.

Within thirty years Thomas had about 1000 followers in forty ecclesias throughout England, Scotland and Wales. In 1869 he named his magazine, *The Christadelphian*. When he died in 1871 Robert Roberts, the English leader, took over as head of the Christadelphian movement.

Beliefs

Christadelphians insist that all their beliefs are based on the Bible and the Bible alone. They do not have their own particular translation like the Jehovah's Witnesses and they encourage each member to study the Bible for themselves. They have Bible reading notes, weekly Bible studies and Bible lectures and will encourage the use of a concordance and Bible dictionaries. Some will use evangelical commentaries as well. Every member will enjoy discussing the Bible with you and will be very polite. They stress that the Bible is one book and that the Old Testament is of equal value with the New Testament.

God

In the past because of Thomas's writings they were said to believe in a God of flesh and bone and many other gods. But today they seem to believe in one God who alone is to be worshipped and who lives in heaven. Their emphasis is on his oneness. They believe the doctrine of the Trinity is not found in the Bible but is a fabrication of the church. The Trinity is 'not a mystery, but a contradiction – a stultification – an impossibility' (Robert Roberts in *Christendom Astray*).

Jesus

They do not believe that Jesus was pre-existent before his birth as a man, therefore he is not eternal. He was an idea or plan in the mind of God, so the references that seem to speak of his pre-existence are only the personification of the purpose of God, like the personification of wisdom in Proverbs 8. He did not become the Christ until he was baptized and he did not become the divine son of God until he was raised from the dead. This is the same as the adoptionist heresy that troubled the early church, namely that Jesus was a man who after his death was given divine status by God.

Their view of the atonement is also different from evangelical Christians. They insist that Jesus, the man, died as a sacrifice on our behalf, but not instead of us. He who was sinless could not pay the penalty we deserve: that is morally reprehensible. He died and by his resurrection became the first-fruits from the dead so that we could follow him and also become 'immortal'. We can become sons of God, too, brothers of Christ.

The Holy Spirit

As they do not believe in the Trinity, Christadelphians say the Spirit is the radiant invisible power or energy from the Father. 'He is an impersonal force who upholds creation and worked miracles through the apostles in New Testament times.' As the scriptures speak of the Holy Spirit in a personal way using the masculine pronoun rather than the neuter, and state that baptism should be in the name of the Father, the Son and the Holy Spirit, their view seems to disagree with the Bible's teaching.

Salvation

In their teaching on salvation, faith alone is not adequate for salvation; belief, baptism and works are also necessary. God can forgive men because of his grace, and save them from extinction at death, if they repent, believe, are baptized and live according to God's law as found in the Bible. Like Jesus, the firstborn from the dead, they too can be raised to immortality. Roberts wrote that 'nothing will save a man in the end but an exact knowledge of the will of God as contained in Scripture, and a faithful carrying out of the same.' This seems an impossibly high standard and helps to explain why they study the Bible so diligently. There can be no assurance of salvation in this teaching.

The Kingdom

At the centre of their beliefs is the kingdom of God. When they pray 'thy kingdom come' they envisage the time when Jesus will return to reign on earth. The Jews will return to Palestine, Israel will be restored, there will be a new temple where sacrifices will be offered again and Jesus will rule from Jerusalem. The faithful, who are believed to have been in soul sleep, will be raised to immortality to join Jesus in his kingdom on earth. Heaven is believed to be only the abode of God and there is no hell, for the wicked are annihilated.

CHRISTIAN SCIENCE

Another church founded over one hundred years ago is the Church of Christ, Scientist. It began in the USA and two-thirds of its branches are still found there. Most of the remaining third are in Britain, and the rest are scattered through Europe, Canada, Australasia and fifty other countries. Many larger towns in Britain have a Christian Science church and in each church area there is a Reading Room where non-members can go and study their publications. In newsagents and on news stands you may see copies of their daily paper *The Christian Science Monitor*. This contains only positive news.

Unlike the Jehovah's Witnesses, the Mormons and the Seventh-Day Adventists, Christian Science is a declining church rather than a growing one. Its membership rose to 300,00 in the 1930s but there are now only 2,000 churches and societies worldwide. It does not publish membership figures but a 'society' will have fewer than fifty members and a 'church' over fifty.

They are best known for their repudiation of professional medicine. Illness does not exist and therefore good health is achieved by the triumph of mind over matter, or more accurately, by right thinking and prayer. Most doctors today would recognize the influence of mental and psychological factors in disease and its treatment, but Christian Scientists rule out physical factors altogether because they maintain that matter is an illusion, it does not exist. Because of their failure at times to achieve this triumph of right thinking, some members will be allowed to have pain-killers or other medical help until they can cope mentally. Others have died rather than accept medical aid.

History

The church was begun by Mary Baker Eddy. She was born into a devout Christian home in America but her father held strong views about predestination, the wrath of God and hell, and seemed to Mary to lack love and compassion. This made her look for other religious ideas and patterns.

She suffered ill health from childhood. Her first husband died soon after they were married and her second husband proved unfaithful. These physical and mental strains led her to seek help from Phineas Quimby, a healer. How much he influenced her is a debated subject but she came to believe in the triumph of mind over matter in questions of health.

Quimby died in 1866 and just over a month later Mary fell on an icy pavement. While confined to bed with a severe back injury she read the story of the paralysed man in Matthew 9:2-8. Believing Jesus was telling her to get out of bed and walk, she got up and found she was miraculously healed. Again there are different views of the story but Mary claims that it was at that time that the basic principles of healing were revealed to her. She began to lecture on healing and continued to study the Bible to establish her beliefs.

In 1875 she published the first edition of her book *Science and Health, with key to the Scriptures*. Christian Scientists claim this book unlocks the hidden secrets of the Bible. After being edited by a retired Unitarian minister, the book was standardized in 1907.

The Church of Christ, Scientist began in 1879 with Mary Baker Eddy as their pastor and in 1892 the mother church, *The First Church of Christ, Scientist*, was established at Boston, Massachusetts. In 1908 their daily newspaper, *The Christian Science Monitor*, began to be produced. But in 1910 Mary Baker Eddy died of pneumonia, aged 89.

The Church and its beliefs today

In 1895 the *Church Manual* was produced setting out the government and practices of the church. Still today Sunday services are led as laid down over one hundred years ago. There are two set readings, one from *Science and Health* and the other from a related passage of the Authorized Version of the Bible, but no preaching, exposition or interpretation is allowed. Public lectures are only given by authorized lecturers. Testimonies are given on Wednesday evenings.

Authority

Although in their basis of faith they claim 'to take the inspired Word of the Bible as our sufficient guide to eternal Life', it has to be read and interpreted according to the writings of Mary Baker Eddy. In *Science and Health* she claims that, in 1866, she 'discovered Christian Science . . . this final revelation of the absolute divine Principle of scientific mental healing' which had been lost by orthodox Christianity.

Spirit and matter

Despite her claim that her ideas were revealed by God she would seem to have been influenced by the prevalent philosophies of the time, based on pantheism (God is all and all is God) and the monism of Hinduism (all is one). God, instead of being the creator of Genesis 1, distinct from his creation, becomes 'the Divine Principle', 'an all-pervading intelligence', 'the Immortal Mind', 'Life', 'Truth', 'Spirit'. Spirit alone exists and spirit is eternal. Matter is not eternal, therefore spirit could not create matter. So matter does not exist, it is merely the product of mortal mind, a human concept. This means that sin, illness and death are products of man's 'Mortal Mind' and don't really exist. Once we can grasp this, then sin and sickness can have no power over us.

Mary Baker Eddy taught that Jesus knew the error of mortal belief – 'he bore our infirmities' – and he was the one man who was able to live knowing the truth. If we, like him, reject the beliefs of Mortal Mind, 'by his stripes we can be healed'. Christian Scientists differentiate between this man, Jesus, and the Christ, the true idea of God. Christ is the truth, the

'Way-shower', who comes to heal sickness and sin through Christian Science.

Salvation and goodness

Christian Scientists see no need for salvation from sin that separates us from God, because sin does not exist. To obtain deliverance from all sorts of evil in our lives we need to have a right understanding of God. That will lead to right thinking which in turn leads to right living. Because of this emphasis on right thought and right understanding Christian Science tends to appeal to people of an intellectual and philosophical bent who want to be of good character. Their basis of faith states, 'we pray for that Mind to be in us which was also in Christ Jesus; to do unto others as we would have them do unto us; and to be merciful, just and pure'.

SEVENTH-DAY ADVENTISM

Broadly speaking, the beliefs of many Seventh-Day Adventists today are in agreement with orthodox Christian teaching: they believe in the Trinity, accepting the deity and incarnation of Jesus, his saving death, resurrection and ascension. Faith is necessary to salvation and is prior to works, and the Bible is accepted as their final authority, the word of God. In 1957 they published a 700-page book, *Seventh-Day Adventists Answer Questions on Doctrine* which made these points clear.

History

This group had its beginnings in the first half of the nineteenth century in the States and are now in almost every country of the world. William Miller was a Baptist who enjoyed studying the Bible along with his concordance. By 1818 he became convinced that Christ would come again in 1843 and he put a date to it, October 10th. Because nothing happened on that day he acknowledged his mistake and changed to October 22nd, 1844. When this prediction also failed he confessed his error and eventually died a disappointed man.

His followers, the Millerites, had begun calling people out of other churches but he denounced this. When his prophecies were not fulfilled they found themselves rejected by other Christians and driven into a closely knit group. In the 1840s this Adventist group was influenced by the Seventh-Day Baptists, who believed that Christians should still observe the fourth commandment. They then became Seventh-Day Adventists, though the name wasn't officially adopted until 1860.

Mrs Ellen White, a lady of many visions and, apparently, the gift of prophecy, took over the leadership of this movement. In 1845 she had a vision of Jesus entering the holy of holies of the heavenly sanctuary. She believed this vision explained the prophecies; that in 1844 what had happened was that Jesus had completed his work of atonement. She taught that Christians who observed Sunday had the mark of the beast on them. For some time her teachings (over forty written works) seemed to be held in as high esteem as scripture and led the group away from mainstream Christianity. SDAs today still consider her a prophet and many accept her writings as 'a continuing and authoritative source of truth.'

Distinctive beliefs

Seventh-Day Adventists disregard the early church's practice of worship on the first day of the week and teach that Christians must observe Saturday as the Sabbath. This has caused serious divisions among Christians overseas when other missionaries had already established a Sunday pattern of Church worship. They no longer teach that salvation depends on this, but expect that in time all Christians will see the truth of the practice.

On the basis of such verses as Daniel 8:14 (see also Hebrews 1:3, 8:1-2 and 9:24) many still believe that Jesus did not enter the heavenly sanctuary until 1844, and then began the second and last phase of his atoning ministry – a work of investigative judgment. Other views peculiar to this church include belief that Michael is the pre-incarnate title of Christ, that the scapegoat of Leviticus 16 is Satan, and that when we die we all sleep in an unconscious state known as 'soul sleep'.

This is an interesting church to study as it shows how easy it is for Christians to be drawn away from mainstream Christianity by a convincing leader. It also points to our responsibility to try to prevent division within the church.

Many Seventh-Day Adventists in Britain, Europe, Asia and Africa are now seeking fellowship and co-operation with other Christian churches. Their basis of faith is orthodox, and so it seems good to encourage this co-operation.

The Church today

This church has always been missionary-minded and although it began in America four out of five members now live outside the States. It produces publications in many languages and makes TV and radio broadcasts. Adventists, although they are not rich people, take tithing very seriously, giving one tenth of their income before tax to the church at home and one tenth to missionary work. This releases finances to run missionary hospitals, clinics and preventive medicine programmes as well as schools and colleges. They recommend healthy eating and prohibit alcohol, tobacco and drugs. Many do not drink tea or coffee or eat meat. They have many Bible colleges because they not only train ministers and missionaries but wish to equip every member to witness.

Tensions within their own church and disagreements with other Christians arise over three main issues. First, in an attempt to preserve their distinctiveness, some Adventists either hold Ellen White's books to be more important than the Bible or they interpret the Bible according to her teachings. Second, there is still a major debate within the movement over justification and sanctification. Generally, it seems that they are noted more for their prohibitions and their good works than for their proclamation of the faith and their assurance of salvation. But this charge could be held against many Christian churches and individuals. The third issue, their claim that the Lord's Day should be observed on Saturday, not Sunday, is the one which has proved most divisive in relations with the rest of the Christian church.

Discussion starters

1. Are there any similarities in the way these three groups started? Who started them and why? How might the Christian churches of that time have avoided these groups beginning or growing? What is there for us to learn from this?

2. If a Christian friend of yours began to attend a Christadelphian ecclesia, which passages of Scripture would you encourage him/her to study in order to understand better the orthodox beliefs about Jesus, the Holy Spirit and the Trinity?

3. How does the biblical teaching about God, creation and man that we find in the early chapters of Genesis differ from the Christian Scientist teaching?

4. Why do you think it would be more effective to give your personal testimony to a Jehovah's Witness or a Christadelphian than to a Mormon or a Christian Scientist?

5. Why did the Seventh-Day Adventists separate from other Christian churches? Which issues do you think were the most important and why?

14

The Unification Church, The Family

THE UNIFICATION CHURCH

Many in Britain first met members of the Unification Church, 'the Moonies', in the mid 1970s. Standing on street corners or in shopping centres they tried to sell us literature, candles or flowers, encouraging us to give donations 'to missionary work'. Then papers and magazines began to publish complaints from parents who believed their children had been stolen by the group. In Britain they tried to sue the *Daily Mail* for libel, but in 1983 in the States their leader, Reverend Moon, was found guilty of tax evasion and was imprisoned. Many young people fled from the group during this time and wrote their stories of escape.

This led to the movement keeping a low profile for some years but Moonies are now to be found again on the streets of our larger towns and cities. Their magazine *Vision* lists nine main centres in England, Wales, Scotland and Eire. They claim that they are not another denomination but a worldwide unification movement working for the salvation of the world. They wish to build a society of goodness, to create one family under God and to unite all religious people in solving the world's problems. It sounds admirable and very different from the media reports.

We need to look at the background of the movement and its beliefs to understand the truth about it.

Origins

Yong Myung Moon was born in 1920 into a large, farming family in Korea. His family were Presbyterians, but when he went to Seoul for high school he joined an unorthodox Pentecostal group. They were awaiting a new Messiah and believed that Korea was the new Jerusalem where this Messiah would be born. At the age of sixteen when praying on a mountainside he had a vision of Jesus Christ informing him that he, Moon, was to complete the restoration of mankind which Jesus had begun 2000 years before. So Moon devoted himself to Bible study and prayer, believing that Christianity was about to be re-born in a way which would unite all denominations. He had many visions where he claimed that God, Jesus, Abraham, Moses, Paul and other Old and New Testament characters spoke to him, as well as founders of other religions like Buddha, Confucius and Muhammad.

After studying engineering in Japan during the Second World War he returned to Korea and had his most important vision of Jesus bowing down to him and calling him Master. He then adopted the name of Sun Myung Moon – meaning 'shining sun and moon' – and founded the 'Broad Sea Church'. In this post-war period he was excommunicated by the Presbyterian Church for his unbiblical teaching and imprisoned by the Communists, but it is not clear whether it was for his faith, for bigamy, or for capitalist business activity.

In 1954 he founded the *Holy Spirit Association for the Unification of World Christianity*. Today the group most often uses the name the *Unification Church*, but also the *Unification Movement* or, since 1997, the *Family Federation*. It runs many projects, each under a different name. In Britain the main centre is at Lancaster Gate in London.

One of Moon's followers wrote down his teaching and in 1957 it was published as *The Divine Principle*. Moon claims that it is God's own interpretation of the Bible, the true code to understand its mystery. During the 1960s his church and his power grew in South Korea. He prospered in secular business and his anti-communist activities won him government support.

His wife had left him in 1954 and in 1960 he married Hak-ja Han, claiming that they were to be the father and mother of the divine family, the true parents. Adam and Eve had been intended by God to be the true parents of the Perfect Family on earth. But Eve had intercourse with Satan and was infected by evil causing the 'spiritual' fall. She then had intercourse with Adam and infected him with evil causing the 'physical' fall. Jesus was the second Adam and was intended to succeed where Adam failed. He was opposed by John the Baptist and let down by the Jews, and so was crucified before he could marry and establish the Perfect Family. Jesus, by his death, achieved 'blood atonement' and by his resurrection as a spirit (compare Luke 24:36-39) he achieved 'spiritual' salvation, but Moon himself needed to come as the third Adam to set up the Perfect Family and give 'physical' salvation.

On God's instructions Moon went to America in 1972. He bought a twenty-five-roomed mansion in New York State, and the forty-two-storey New Yorker Hotel as the church offices. On a tour of the major cities he recruited followers, mainly young people, intelligent, well-to-do, Jewish or nominally Christian with a respect for the Bible but no thorough knowledge of it. The movement became more organized and missionaries were sent out to ninety-five different countries. Their aim was to increase the numbers of the Perfect Family through fervent evangelism and public service.

By 1978 Moon claimed there were 360,000 members in Korea in 935 churches, 30,000 in the USA, 6,000 in Germany, 3,000 in Great Britain and over three million members worldwide. More accurate figures were thought to be about 10,000 in Korea in 172 churches, 10,000 in the USA, and only 500 to 1000 in Britain. In their websites today they do not give membership statistics, but rather the numbers attending their special wedding blessings or conferences.

Practices

Drugs and smoking are banned in the movement and continual hard work is enforced in order to avoid sin. Each member is expected to begin by selling literature or small articles like candles or flowers on street corners, in shopping centres, at railway stations or wherever there are crowds of people. They ask for money for missionary work, youth camps or children's charities. But since the court case with the *Daily Mail* they may also come straight out with who they are.

They invite young people who are lonely or in a strange town to a meeting or a meal, showing them great love and concern. Once welcomed at the local centre they are invited to weekend camps and house-parties. They begin to teach them about the Unification Movement and Moon's teachings from The Divine Principle. If recruits originally come in pairs they separate them and put pressure on them to stay, assuring each that the other is happy.

The young recruits, usually from middle-class backgrounds, are persuaded to part from their families, to give up their property and their money to the movement and to work for the cause. As in other groups which began in the 1970s they were then overworked, underfed and deprived of sleep. To make the local community well disposed towards them they are encouraged to baby-sit or dig gardens. They are taught that if they leave the group they go outside God's purposes for them. As God has chosen Moon to unite everyone, if you leave his family you go back to the evil world system and God will judge you. One ex-Moonie said that when she entered a church after leaving the group she expected the roof to fall on her. Many have frightening nightmares for years after they leave.

The movement arranges inter-faith services. When Moonies first came to Britain they applied to join the local council of churches but they were turned down. The Archbishop of Canterbury and other church leaders spoke out against them. Moon also organizes peace conferences, – for example the World Peace Blessing held at the UN in New York in January 2001 – yet much of his wealth has been gained from armament factories. Large international conferences are arranged on scientific, cultural, economic or political subjects. Many members of Parliament and other well-known people have been invited to attend or speak at such conferences or meetings, only to discover when they get there that it is a platform for the Moonies' views and their names have been used to encourage the general public to attend. This is all part of what Moon called 'heavenly deception', which seems similar to the old idea that the ends justify the means. The organization has gone by over fifty different names in Britain alone. Lying, stealing, asking for money under false pretences, and tax evasion are, under some circumstances, seen as legitimate means to further God's work. The world is evil so its laws do not apply to God's people.

Beliefs

Authority

In this movement Moon and his teaching in *The Divine Principle* have become the sole sources of authority. He claims to have direct visions of Jesus, John the Baptist and others that give him this authority. He teaches his followers, 'I am the thinker; I am your brain.' There is no need for them to use their own minds to search the Scriptures and wrestle with biblical truth.

God

As in Eastern religions, in Mormonism and in Christian Science, the biblical distinction between God and man is lost. Moon has said, 'He [God] is living in me and I am in the incarnation of him.' 'God and man are one. Man is incarnate God.' When men reach perfection they can become as God. He denies that the God of the Bible is in sovereign control of the world, for God makes plans and they do not work. In the Old Testament he contradicts himself for there are prophecies that Jesus will succeed and be victorious and others that he will suffer and die. His followers are taught to pray to God, but not through Jesus, rather through 'our true parents, Sun Myung Moon, and his wife, our Mother'. 'Jesus is a man in whom God is incarnate, not God himself.' Moon's teaching is that Jesus can become a second god because he was sinless, but through his death he achieved only blood atonement and through his resurrection only spiritual salvation.

The Lord of the Second Advent

Moon writes much about 'the Lord of the Second Advent', a second messiah – another anointed one. With his wife, this messiah will finally establish the true family of God in which physical salvation is to be found. Since God took about 2000 years from the time of Abraham to prepare for the first messiah, Moon teaches that the second messiah will arrive about 2000 years later. He has been born in the East, as prophesied in Revelation 7:2-3, in about 1920, but not in China because it is communist, not in Japan because it persecuted Christians in Korea, but in Korea. Moon has never directly said he is the Lord of the Second Advent, though in 1992 he declared publicly that he and his wife are the messiah and the True Parents of all humanity. His followers believe he is 'the Lord of the Second Advent' and that salvation is only to be found by being adopted into his family.

The faithful will only enter the Kingdom of heaven in families so marriage is very important. Marriages are arranged among the members of the movement. Divorce is only allowed if one partner leaves the movement. Sex outside marriage is frowned upon, there is no sympathy for illegitimate children and long periods of sexual abstinence are expected within marriage. In February 1999 the largest simultaneous wedding in history was held. The main ceremony was in the Seoul Olympic Stadium. 360 million couples of different faiths and cultures from 193 nations took part in centres all over the world. Some were marrying for the first time and others were renewing their marriage vows.

The strong anti-communist stance of the group has been dropped since the breaking down of the Berlin Wall and they have lost no time in moving into Russia and Eastern Europe to gain new members.

Christian witness

Many of us will meet Moonies in the street but it does not help to say you are a Christian or to give your testimony. They are trained to agree with you and will not discuss anything with you there. It is not advisable to go to their centres or training courses because a great deal of psychological pressure will be put on you. One psychologist who did go was drawn into the movement! It is better to ask them questions about their past. 'How long have you been in the movement?' 'What did you do before you joined?' Ask them questions about their schooling, the place where they grew up or their parents. Often they have lost touch with the real world and need to be put back in touch.

Do not call them 'Moonies' or insult their founder. If you are going to help them it will need to be in the context of long-term friendship. If you do meet a member who is willing to talk with you, invite him or her to your home. As marriage is so fundamental to their understanding of salvation, a happy Christian marriage or family will impress them. You can offer them a New Testament but they may be too busy to read it. Often they work in pairs or teams so you may find it difficult to strike up contact with any one person. All will need to be done in prayer because you will be entering a spiritual battle.

THE FAMILY

A group called the Children of God emerged from the hippy movement in the States during the 1960s. In 1978 the group changed its name to the Family of Love. More recently they have styled themselves the Family, or the Fellowship of Independent Missionary Communities.

In 1966 some drug-taking dropouts in California became believers in Jesus. They began to run coffee bars and reached out evangelistically to their contemporaries who had renounced the established, materialistic way of life of their parents' generation. In a strong movement of the Holy Spirit many of these young people came to Christ, but they did not feel at home in, nor were they accepted by, the conventional churches. They set up Christian communes, maintaining their simple, radical lifestyle and continuing to witness to other dropouts. Through their influence hundreds of thousands of young people followed Jesus. They were labelled as 'The Jesus People' or 'the Jesus Movement' or, less charitably, 'the Jesus Freaks'.

Origins

Many of the young people have since become members and leaders in mainline churches and missions. Others set up new fellowships or missions which have now become accepted branches of the Christian church. The Children of God was one group that began in that era of youth revival. It was founded by David Berg. He was born in 1919 to parents who were both evangelists of the Christian and Missionary Alliance church. He became a pastor of one of their churches in Arizona. In 1949 he said that his views over issues of racial integration, wealth and poverty became too radical for his church leaders to stomach, so he left disillusioned with the established church. He went to South California to work with Fred Jordan, a Pentecostal pastor with a radio and TV ministry. In 1968 he began a ministry called 'teens for Christ' based on a coffee house. He expected all new converts to give up their jobs, adopt a communal lifestyle and study the Bible for six to eight hours a day.

A year later at the age of fifty he prophesied that California was going to suffer a severe earthquake and be covered by the sea. So, like Moses before him, he led his people out into the desert. He called himself Moses David and his 150 followers became known as the Children of God.

While on a visit to Montreal in Canada he organized his followers into twelve tribes and gave them all biblical names. He had begun to have a sexual relationship with his secretary, Maria, and he justified it on the grounds that she was a symbol of the new church (Children of God) approved by God, and that his wife, Jane, was a symbol of the old church.

At this stage he was still teaching the biblical doctrine of salvation by grace and sending his followers out to witness to the necessity of an encounter with Jesus. So Fred Jordan invited Berg and his group to make their base on his ranch in Texas and to be involved in outreach in California. He raised money for them through his radio and TV programmes. Then came reports of kidnapping, brainwashing and fraud so in September 1971 Jordan disassociated himself from Berg and banned the Children of God from his property. Over 2000 of them scattered, splitting into more than forty 'colonies'. The colony that came to England was warmly welcomed by some influential evangelical Christians because its members preached the gospel and adopted a radical lifestyle.

In 1973 Berg prophesied that the comet Kahoutek would cause the destruction of America the following year unless there was national repentance. This prophecy proved false and in September of that year the Charity Frauds Bureau of New York State reported to the State attorney that there was evidence of tax evasion, kidnapping, indoctrination and sexual perversion in the group. This led to a mass exodus from America and the formation of colonies, each of twelve people, in many countries. In 2001 they claim to have 12,000 full-time adult members in over 100 countries.

Practices

This group was better known for its practices than its beliefs. It was difficult to identify their beliefs because they changed during the 1970s and '80s with each new 'Mo Letter'. Berg, alias Moses David, wrote these letters, some for the general public, some for his disciples or friends and others for committed members of the group. These were to be studied by his followers for one and a half to two hours each day. He also wrote special letters for the members of his own family, 'the Royal Family', who ruled the groups under him. One son died in Switzerland in 1973 and his daughter, Linda, left the group in 1978. In 1984 her book *The Children of God – The Inside Story* was published.

The Children of God began as a Bible-based group, but committed to one leader and to a radical, commune-style way of life. Before long the source of authority had passed from the Bible to the directive letters of its charismatic, authoritarian leader. He alone gave the correct interpretation of Scripture and until his death in 1994 he alone ruled the lives of the members through his enforced hierarchical structure.

From the start Berg was opposed to the established churches and other Christians, except when he wished to obtain money or converts. Later on he said that only his followers were the true disciples of Christ and other churches were like the world system, 'of the devil'. But on the question of hell he is, rather unexpectedly, a universalist, believing that almost everyone will be saved after death and judgment. Only a few exceptionally wicked people will join Satan in hell.

Moses David Berg's own perverse sexual practices led him to encourage free love, homosexuality, lesbianism and paedophilia among his followers. Girls were told to practise 'flirty fishing', to become 'hookers for Jesus', that is to seduce men, making love with them to show how much God loves them. Even the Holy Spirit is pictured in their literature as a seductive female figure. Jesus was said to be the product of physical intercourse between God and Mary. He was also said to have had intercourse with at least two women – Mary Magdalene and Mary the sister of Martha, and to have contracted venereal disease in order to have 'full compassion' on the sufferings of those who have such diseases! Since the publicity about AIDS, however, the group has been changing its practices.

The Family has many similarities to the Moonies. Converts are expected to become childishly dependent on their spiritual superiors. 'Babes', as new recruits are called, are not given all the teaching at once but drawn in gently. They are expected to give up all their privacy, freedom and income to 'the Family' and are told to ask their relatives for money too.

Ordinary witnessing was abandoned in favour of 'litnessing', raising money by selling literature. Full members are encouraged to do this for ten hours a day. Deceit, lies and stealing are permitted, as well as sexual licence, because no action is wrong in itself; it depends whether it is done 'in the flesh' or 'in the spirit'.

'Moses' Berg's first two prophecies of judgment on California and on the USA proved false, but he still claimed to be a prophet. In the 1980s he made false prophecies that there would be a communist takeover of the world in which Russia would defeat Israel at Armageddon. Seven years later in 1993 he claimed Christ would come again. These prophecies have not been fulfilled.

There is a strong element of spiritism in Berg's teaching. Soon after he left California he began to be guided by a spirit medium, Abrahim. Many of his Mo Letters claim to be written with the help of his numerous spirit-guides. Through these guides he claimed to have the wisdom of the ages sent to him by God. He encouraged his followers to be involved with the occult and spiritism and he even claimed to have sex with spirits. Occult activity is forbidden by God in the biblical record (eg Deuteronomy 18:10-13; 1 Chronicles 10:13-14; Isaiah 8:19-20), though Berg maintained that being 'spiritual' meant getting in touch with spirits.

Berg redefined other biblical terms too, giving them an unbiblical meaning. Perhaps the most devastating was his use of the word 'love'; in his teachings the *agape* love of the Bible became *eros* – sexual love.

In the sermon on the mount (Matthew 7:15-23) Jesus warns his disciples of false prophets, and says, 'by their fruit you will recognize them'. Berg's prophecies proved false, and his lifestyle did not demonstrate the fruit of the Spirit of which the New Testament speaks. If you consult their website you will see that they claim to be biblical Christians who desire to preach the gospel and to show Christ's love to the needy. However, they still use all the Mo letters with their highly imaginative and devious teaching.

Christian witness

If we wish to help any people who belong to unorthodox groups to come to an orthodox faith in Jesus Christ we will need to know our own beliefs well and be able to express them clearly. But first of all we will have to listen to them and hear and understand what they are saying; not all members of a church will share exactly the same beliefs. Some Christians have even been known to correct members of these groups saying, 'But you are supposed to believe. . .' ! Listen to them, let them tell you what they believe, but pray that the Holy Spirit will show you what to say. Also pray that the Holy Spirit will give them a dissatisfaction with what they have and open their hearts to the truth of God in Jesus Christ. No amount of arguing, verbal persuasion, theology degrees or in-depth study of cults will bring a person to the truth unless God's Holy Spirit is convincing him or her.

More important than anything you say will be your life. Do the fruits of the Holy Spirit show in your life? Can the other person see that your beliefs have changed you and are changing you? Does he see love, patience, kindness in your relationship with him and others? Or does he see pride, prejudice and a pushing of your beliefs onto others? Do you read and know your Bible or do you just repeat what others have taught you? Does your life point to a God who is loving and merciful, slow to anger and of great kindness?

You will need to be clear in your own mind about which Christian beliefs are basic to life and salvation and which are peripheral, and why. When a friend is becoming involved in a religious group that deviates from orthodox Christianity and asks you what you think, you will need to be able to point him, graciously and clearly, to passages in Scripture that teach about the nature of God, the person and work of Jesus, the meaning of salvation and eternal life.

Those who leave such a group need to do so as a result of their own decision: they cannot be forced into it. They will need much long-term care and love, not instant re-programming. Do not push them into attending church or Bible study groups or into 'making a decision for Christ.' Neither should you run down the movement they have just left. Listen to them, talk with them personally about Jesus when they are ready, and above all pray for them.

Discussion starters

1. What do you think are the main errors of these groups?

2. Why do you think a young person might join a group like the Moonies or the Children of God? Share any stories or testimonies you have read or heard which tell you why a person joined.

3. In 1971 an organization called FREE-COG was set up by shocked and irate parents in the USA to work together to free their children from the group. Since then some parents have resorted to kidnapping and de-programming to bring their children out of such groups. When Linda Berg wished her own daughter to leave the Family of Love she flew to South America and spoke with her there, but did not force her to return. Why do you think she chose that approach? What can parents do to help in these situations?

4. What makes it difficult for anyone to leave a religious group such as the two we have been considering in this chapter?

5. When someone leaves or wants to leave what will Christians need to do to help the person?

15

How can we witness?

If we are at all concerned for our neighbours we will want to share our discovery of Christ with them, particularly if they are locked into a way of life or system of beliefs which seems to take them further away from him. An accurate knowledge of their faith is crucial to our understanding of them, but once armed with this knowledge there are three main ways in which we can approach them with news of Jesus.

Loving Friendship

A Sikh child feels lonely and isolated – the only boy with a turban in the school playground.

A young woman of Indian origin, born and brought up in Britain and just finishing a course at a British college, faces the prospect of an arranged marriage to a man she has never met.

An Asian family lives in a tower block where they constantly face racial harassment and violence from a gang of violent white youths.

A group of bored West Indian lads stands on the street corner. There are no jobs for them and they feel as though they have been put at the bottom of the pile.

An acquaintance of yours used to go to church but she is now very involved with the local Kingdom Hall.

One thing which none of these people are likely to reject, is friendship. Some of them, indeed, are very much in need of it.

It is crucial that Christians go out of their way to befriend those who do not belong to the Christian 'flock', particularly those of other religions who may be contending with an alien culture. Jesus described himself as the 'good shepherd' who would leave his own secure environment and strike out into unfamiliar, maybe even hostile, territory to find the sheep that had got lost. Jesus' followers need the same attitude of outgoing self-sacrificing love.

Be hospitable, particularly to those from other cultures. Invite them into your home for tea, coffee, or a meal. To be on the safe side, offer them only vegetarian food. Many Asians in Britain have never been invited into the homes of their white neighbours!

As Christians we must take the lead in opposing all racial prejudice and discrimination. Sadly, we still see evidence of racist attitudes in the church and we must therefore correct ourselves first. The love of Christ makes all such attitudes a grave sin which must not be allowed to continue among us. The church as a body, and Christians individually, cannot have any true or effective witness among the ethnic minorities unless we are seen to have overcome racial prejudice and pride.

This will undoubtedly lead us into deeper involvement with our society as a whole.

Local schools, polytechnics and universities need to be prayed for, visited, and helped in practical ways. Many students live surprisingly isolated lives, particularly in the bigger cities, and are susceptible to the teachings of cults which offer so much else. We need to offer them the support and encouragement necessary to maintain their self-confidence and discernment. There is also much that local groups of churches can do to establish job training and employment initiatives.

In all this, friendship and practical help must not just be a cover for trying to convert people. It is important that our friendship should be on equal terms, not the strong offering paternalistic charity to the weak. Friendship means genuine sharing, and real enjoyment and appreciation of each other. Friends like to relax and do things together, to visit each other's homes, to share the problems and the good things of life.

Conversation

At the end of Chapter One we saw that our witness is not only to be through the visual testimony of our lives, but also by our words. We are to 'preach' the gospel – and preaching is not done only from a pulpit or soapbox, but equally by chatting over a shop counter or across a garden fence.

Our verbal witness will include a lot of listening as well as talking. Only then can we know what our friends are understanding by what we say. Do they hear what we think we are saying? It is only when we have listened and learned that we can share the good news of Jesus in a way that is relevant and appropriate. It is also just basic politeness to listen to the other person's views rather than thrusting our own beliefs down their throats. Our 'preaching' will therefore be more by discussion together than by sermon!

When discussing religious issues and the claims of Jesus Christ, it is vital that we avoid heated argument. If we win the argument we shall probably lose our friendship and may make that friend actually hostile to any further approaches from Christians. Likewise, we should avoid trying to compete over which religion has the 'best' historical record. It is easy to slip into the trap and begin to boast of how Christians initiated, for instance, the freeing of slaves. We love to show how it was Christian missions who laid the foundations for medical care in so many countries and also started their educational processes. Other religions can also boast of good things in their history – and can point an accusing finger at some awful Christian failures, like the Crusades or colonial and imperial history.

I once showed a nominal Christian Englishman round the main mosque in Singapore. A Muslim joined us and immediately began to tell us how rotten Christianity is and how lovely Islam is. I could see my friend getting increasingly annoyed. Then the Muslim claimed that Christians never really pray in churches because they allow women to be in the congregation, so the men just think lustfully about the girls. My friend exploded, angrily telling the Muslim that Islam must be corrupt if its men cannot sit in the presence of girls without continually lusting in their minds! He then told the Muslim how Christianity so changes men's hearts that our thoughts are purified. He sounded like a very committed Christian, but actually he wasn't. If the Muslim had been a little more humble about Islam and more gracious about the Christian faith, my friend would have been more open to learn from his witness. As it was, he became defensive. We Christians also often need to learn this lesson.

It can be helpful to start a conversation with someone from another faith by asking questions. What do they believe about the afterlife? How do they get strength to overcome temptation? What is their experience of prayer? What does their sense of religious community mean in practice? Some may also want to ask more theological questions, like: 'What do you believe about the nature of man?' or 'What do you think God is like?' One can learn a lot by listening to the answers to such questions. It is a way to begin to enter into the feelings and beliefs of other people. Very often they will ask you in return what you as a Christian believe and experience. This will allow you not only to give the theory of the Christian faith, but also your own personal testimony.

When you share your own experience of conversion and the Christian life, be honest and realistic. It is easy to slip into 'shaving cream advertisement testimony'. The shaving cream advertisement shows a picture of a man's face covered with unshaven bristles and looking distinctly unattractive – but that was 'BEFORE'. The second picture shows the same face lathered by several inches of shaving cream. The third picture shows the man beaming with a satisfied smile, his skin gleaming, and smooth as velvet. This is 'AFTER'. Above the whole sequence of pictures stands the motto, 'Use Bloggs' shaving cream'! We sometimes testify as if our pre-Christian experience was all 'sin and misery' but then, after we had been 'redeemed by the blood of Jesus', we came into 'full salvation'. Sin was 'cleansed', life 'renewed', problems 'solved', all became 'full of joy and peace'. Of course there is some truth in such a testimony, but it is not the whole truth. And if we use those sorts of words or phrases to describe it we will, at best, be met with blank incomprehension and, at worst, be completely misunderstood. As Christians we are still far from perfect and we still live in the real world. So be honest in describing your Christian experience, and be careful to speak about it in normal, everyday language.

There are many opportunities for sharing at this level with people of non-European backgrounds. Europeans have largely pushed religion off the centre of the stage and now find it hard to talk about spiritual matters in public, but most other cultures still reckon that religion is central to daily life. They will often talk easily and naturally about God and religion, so it is easy to enter into conversation and discussion on such issues.

Discussion will often stem from a natural curiosity about each other's religion. Many British young people sense their ignorance about other religions and would be fascinated to have the chance to visit a temple or mosque to see for themselves what they are like. People of other faiths might also appreciate the opportunity to attend a church service or some other Christian activity in order to understand Christianity better.

If we are going to encourage such interchange, the Christian will need to pray. Before going to a temple or mosque it is vital to know the protective covering of Christ, so that we do not leave ourselves open to demonic attack. We shall also want to pray that on our friend's return visit to our Christian service he or she will sense the reality and attractive, life-giving beauty of our Lord Jesus.

It may sometimes be helpful not only to invite our non-Christian friend to visit our church with us, but also to ask him to come to a small meeting either at the church or in someone's home to tell us about his faith or his home country. By asking him to speak to us we may avoid the danger of that condescending paternalism which we have already noted.

Good books

As Christians we believe that the Bible is God's word to mankind. Hebrews 4:12 affirms that 'the word of God is living and active'. It is through the Bible that we came, ultimately, to a knowledge of Jesus as our Saviour and as Lord, so we shall want to encourage our friends to read the Bible for themselves.

The Bible is, however, a big book and it is sometimes hard to see the wood for the trees. For years I read the Bible without understanding what it was really saying. Even the God-fearing Ethiopian eunuch needed Philip to explain Isaiah 53 to him (Acts 8:30-31). So guide your friend to the bits of the Bible you suggest he reads first and help him to understand what he reads. In many cases it may prove best to start with one of the Gospels, perhaps Luke, and then go on to Acts. If your friend is a Hindu or Sikh, the Gospel of John will be most appropriate.

It is good also to lend other Christian books. Some may want to know what Christianity is really all about and then it will be right to lend them a basic book of Christian teaching. Others may not be ready for anything so heavy yet and will prefer an interesting biography which illustrates what it means to live as a Christian. My wife sometimes takes a book like that to read when having her hair done, enthuses about it to the hairdresser and then lends it to her!

Conclusion

When we begin to befriend and witness to people of other faiths, we shall quickly discover that some are very open to the gospel while others are strongly resistant. With some, therefore, it may be possible to share the basics of the gospel quite quickly and with a high expectation that they will come to faith in Jesus Christ. With others we will need to be very patient and not be discouraged when they seem closed to our witness.

With some notable exceptions we shall find that Muslims react strongly against any idea that they might become Christians. On the other hand some Muslims from Iran have become quite disillusioned about their faith and a steady trickle are becoming Christians today. Some African and Indonesian Muslims are also quite open to Jesus Christ. But Muslims from the Middle East and North Africa will test both our patience and our steadfast love.

At the other end of the spectrum many Chinese people, Africans and international students are today quite predisposed towards the message of Jesus if it is shared with them in a relevant and committed manner.

But whether people are relatively open to the gospel or not, it is our responsibility as Christians to love our neighbours as ourselves and so share with them all that is precious to us, particularly the good news of life and salvation in Jesus Christ.

This is God's work and Satan will do his utmost to thwart it. It is ultimately a spiritual battle which we can only win through persistent and believing prayer.

Discussion starters

1. What people of other faiths do you have in your school, college or place of work? Have they grown up in the country or are they new to it? What particular problems might they be facing? What can you do to help?

2. Find someone of another faith and discuss with them how you both view marriage, parents, children, religion, prayer, death and the afterlife.

3. Do you sometimes find racial prejudice coming into your thinking or behaviour? What makes you, or others, think this way? What does the Bible have to say about this?

4. What fruits of the Spirit (see Galatians 5:22-23) are specially necessary in witness to those from religious movements and from other religions?

5. It is sometimes difficult to keep up friendships with non-Christians once we become Christians. Should you think about spending less time in church activities, and more time getting to know non-Christians locally?

6. If you do not have friends or acquaintances among people of other religions or deviant Christian beliefs, do you think you should try to meet and befriend some? Why or why not? If you wish to, how will you go about doing so?

Further Reading

Basic reading on Chapters 1 and 2

Wright, C.J.H., *Thinking Clearly About the Uniqueness of Jesus*. Monarch, 1997.

Judaism

Epstein, I., *Judaism*. Harmondsworth: Penguin, 1970.
Jessup, G., *No Strange God*. London: Olive Press 1976.
Wouk, H., *This Is My God*. London: Fontana, 1976.

Islam

Ali, M. Nazir, *Islam – A Christian Perspective*. Paternoster, 1983.
Cooper, A., *Ishmael My Brother*. Bromley: MARC Europe, 1985.
Goldsmith, M., *Islam and Christian Witness*: Bromley: MARC Europe, 1987.
Goldsmith, M., *Islam and Christian Witness*. OM Paternoster, 1991.
Moucarry, C., *Faith To Faith, Christianity and Islam in Dialogue*. IVP, 2001.

Hinduism

Maharaj, R., *Death of a Guru*. London: Hodder and Stoughton, 1986.
Burnett, D., *The Spirit of Hinduism*. Monarch, 1992.

Gidoomal, R., and Fearon, M., *Karma 'n' Chips, The New Age of Asian Spirituality*. Wimbledon Publishing, 1988.

Gidoomal, R., *Chapatis for Tea – Reseaching Your Hindu Neighbour – A Practical Guide*. Highland Books, 1994.

Klostermaier, K., *A Short Introduction to Hinduism*. Oxford: One World Publications, 1998.

Sen, K., *Hinduism*. Harmondsworth: Penguin, 1970.

Sikhism

Cole, W. Owen and Sambhi, P., *The Sikhs: Their Religious Beliefs and Practices*. London: Routledge, 1978.

Buddhism

Burnett, D., *The Spirit of Buddhism: A Christian Perspective on Buddhist Thought*. Monarch, 1998.

Carrithers, M., *The Buddha*. Oxford: Oxford University Press, 1983.

Klostermaier, K., *Buddhism, a Short Introduction*. Oxford: One World Publications, 1999.

Swearer, D., *Buddhism*. Harlow: Argus Communications, 1978.

Williams, P., *Mahayana Buddhism, The Doctrinal Foundaions*. Routledge, 1989.

Traditional Chinese and Japanese Religions

Dawson, R., *Confucius*. Oxford: Oxford University Press, 1981.

Nelson, J.K., *Enduring Identities – The Guise of Shinto In Contemporary Japan*. University of Hawaii Press, 2000.

Palmer, M., *The Elements of Taoism*. Element, 1991.

Thompson, L.G., *Chinese Religions – An Introduction*. Wadsworth Publishing Co., 1996.

General

The Lion Handbook of The World's Religions. Tring: Lion, 1984.

Suggested addition:

Glaser, I & Raja, S., *Sharing the Salt, Making Friends with Sikhs, Muslims and Hindus*. Milton Keynes: Scripture Union, 1999.

Books on the new religious movements

Barker, E., *New Religious Movements: A Practical Introduction*. London: HMSO, 1989.

Barrett, D.V., *Sects, 'Cults' and Alternative Religions*. London: Cassell, 2000.

Martin, W., *Kingdom of the Cults*. Minneapolis: Bethany, 1992; *New Cults*. Ventura: Regal, 1985.

Melton, J.G., *Encyclopedic Handbook of Cults in America*. New York/London: Garland, 1992

Tucker, R., *Another Gospel*. Grand Rapids: Zondervan, 1989.

Wilson, B.R., *The Social Dimensions of Sectarianism, Sects and New Religious Movements in Contemporary Society*. Oxford: Clarendon, 1990

Wilson, B.R., (ed.), *New Religious Movements, Challenge and Response*. London: Routledge, 1999.

Wookey, S., *When a Church Becomes a Cult*. London: Hodder & Stoughton, 1996.

It is also good to consult the original writings of a group and their websites if you wish to understand their thinking more fully.

Books on basic Christian doctrine

The following books on basic Christian doctrine are all published by Scripture Union. They provide short, practical summaries of orthodox Christian belief.

The Trinity

Macleod, D., *Shared Life* (1987).

God

Grayston, J., *God* (1986).

Jesus

Cooke, F., *Jesus* (1984).
Evans, M., *God In Our Shoes* (1987).
Sproul, R.C., *Who Is Jesus?* (1986).

The Holy Spirit

Calver, C., *The Holy Spirit* (1984).

Mankind

Jackman, D., *Humanity* (1986).

Salvation

Barrs, J., *The Great Rescue* (1989).
Forster, R., *Saving Faith* (1984).

The Bible

Eddison, J., *The Bible* (1984).

The Ascension and Second Coming

Baxter, C., *Ready For The Party?* (1987).

General books on Christian belief

Cotterell, P., *This Is Christianity*. Leicester: IVP, 1985.
Gaukroger, S., *It Makes Sense*. London: Scripture Union, 1987.
Keeley, R. (ed.), *The Lion Handbook of Christian Belief*. Tring: Lion, 1982.

Keeley, R. (ed.), *The Lion Handbook of Christianity: A World Faith*. Tring: Lion, 1985.
Wood, M., *This Is Our Faith*. London: Hodder and Stoughton, 1985.

English-speaking OMF centres

AUSTRALIA: PO Box 849, Epping, NSW 2121
Freecall 1800 227 154. email: omf-australia@omf.net. *www.omf.org*

CANADA: 5759 Coopers Avenue, Mississauga ON, L4Z 1R9
Toll free 1-888-657-8010. email: omfcanada@omf.ca. *www.omf.ca*

HONG KONG: PO Box 70505, Kowloon Central Post Office, Hong Kong. email: hk@omf.net. *www.omf.org*

MALAYSIA: 3A Jalan Nipah, off Jalan Ampang, 55000, Kuala Lumpur. email: my@omf.net. *www.omf.org*

NEW ZEALAND: PO Box 10159, Dominion Road, Auckland 1030
Tel 9-630 5778. email: omfnz@omf.net. *www.omf.org*

PHILIPPINES: 900 Commonwealth Avenue, Diliman, 1101 Quezon City. email: ph-hc@omf.net. *www.omf.org*

SINGAPORE: 2 Cluny Road, Singapore 259570
email: sno@omf.net. *www.omf.org*

SOUTHERN AFRICA: PO Box 3080, Pinegowrie, 2123
email: za@omf.net.*www.omf.org*

UK: Station Approach, Borough Green, Sevenoaks, Kent, TN15 8BG
Tel 01732 887299. email: omf@omf.org.uk. *www.omf.org.uk*

USA: 10 West Dry Creek Circle, Littleton, CO 80120-4413
Toll Free 1-800-422-5330. email: omf@omf.org. *www.us.omf.org*

OMF International Headquarters:
2 Cluny Road, Singapore 259570